LEBRON JAMES

LEBRON JAMES

A Biography

Lew Freedman

GREENWOOD BIOGRAPHIES

GREENWOOD PRESS
WESTPORT, CONNECTICUT • LONDON

Library of Congress Cataloging-in-Publication Data

Freedman, Lew.
    LeBron James : a biography / Lew Freedman.
        p. cm. — (Greenwood biographies, ISSN 1540–4900)
    Includes bibliographical references and index.
    ISBN 978–0–313–34361–2 (alk. paper)
  1. James, LeBron.   2. Basketball players—United States—Biography.
I. Title.
    GV884.J36F74   2008
    796.323092—dc22
    [B]   2007048841

British Library Cataloguing in Publication Data is available.

Library of Congress Catalog Card Number: 2007048841

ISBN: 978–0–313–34361–2
ISSN: 1540–4900

First published in 2008

Greenwood Press, 88 Post Road West, Westport, CT 06881
An imprint of Greenwood Publishing Group, Inc.
www.greenwood.com

Printed in the United States of America

The paper used in this book complies with the
Permanent Paper Standard issued by the National
Information Standards Organization (Z39.48–1984).

10 9 8 7 6 5 4 3 2 1

CONTENTS

Photo essay follows page 80

SERIES FOREWORD

In response to high school and public library needs, Greenwood developed this distinguished series of full-length biographies specifically for student use. Prepared by field experts and professionals, these engaging biographies are tailored for high school students who need challenging yet accessible biographies. Ideal for secondary school assignments, the length, format, and subject areas are designed to meet educators' requirements and students' interests.

Greenwood offers an extensive selection of biographies spanning all curriculum related subject areas including social studies, the sciences, literature and the arts, history and politics, as well as popular culture, covering public figures and famous personalities from all time periods and backgrounds, both historical and contemporary, who have made an impact on American and/or world culture. Greenwood biographies are chosen based on comprehensive feedback from librarians and educators. Consideration was given to both curriculum relevance and inherent interest. The result is an intriguing mix of the well known and the unexpected, the saints and sinners from long-ago history and contemporary pop culture. Readers will find a wide array of subject choices from fascinating crime figures like Al Capone to inspiring pioneers like Margaret Mead, from the greatest minds of our time like Stephen Hawking to the most amazing success stories of our day like J. K. Rowling.

While the emphasis is on fact, not glorification, the books are meant to be fun to read. Each volume provides in-depth information about the subject's life from birth through childhood, the teen years, and adulthood.

A thorough account relates family background and education, traces personal and professional influences, and explores struggles, accomplishments, and contributions. A timeline highlights the most significant life events against a historical perspective. Bibliographies supplement the reference value of each volume.

ACKNOWLEDGMENTS

Thank you to the writers who came before me and studied and reported on basketball star LeBron James's life and career before and during his rise to prominence.

It was especially illuminating to read books about different aspects of James's life by B.J. Robinson, Roger Gordon, David Lee Morgan, and Ryan Jones and stories written about James and the Cleveland Cavaliers in the *Akron Beacon-Journal* and *Cleveland Plain Dealer*.

The public relations staff of the Cleveland Cavaliers was very helpful, as well.

INTRODUCTION

It was two hours to game time at the Quicken Loans Arena in downtown Cleveland on a mild November night at the beginning of the 2006–07 National Basketball Association season. The Cleveland Cavaliers were hosting the Atlanta Hawks. A ritual unfolded in the hallway outside of the Cavs' dressing room.

Newspaper, radio, and television reporters gathered at a selected spot and waited. It was the daily welcoming committee, a part of the "LeBron Rules." LeBron James, the young star of the Cavaliers, was so popular and in such demand that the player and his team established a protocol designed to prevent him from becoming verbally besieged.

If left to their own devices and inclinations, reporters would flock to James seeking private one-on-one moments, leaving him no time for game preparation, no time for warm-ups, no time to think. LeBron, who should be the next president? LeBron, what should the ending of "The Sopranos" be? LeBron, should the United States pull out of Iraq tomorrow? The player would squirm. The sessions would deteriorate into levels of silliness normally reserved for Saturday morning cartoons.

So the Cavaliers' public relations crew and James created a pregame routine to allow the player to focus on playing and yet provide suitable access to the men and women covering his still burgeoning basketball career. The agreed-upon solution was for James to speak with reporters before each game for a short while as soon as he entered the building. Then it was understood that he was off-limits for questions until after the games.

What evolved was essentially a pleasant bantering session between James and the media. James was at ease, the reporters asked what they wished, and for the most part there was little tension or controversy. James was practiced at this type of encounter, often cracked jokes, and frequently charmed his listeners. Much like a successful stand-up comic, he often left them laughing and wanting more.

In an era when professional athletes are often seen as aloof, spoiled, and bored with daily media attention, James presented himself as the poster child for the cooperative superstar, the anti-grump. It was easy to forget at the start of his fourth professional season that he was not yet 22 years old, that he was barely more than three years removed from high school.

But in an America that manufactures new heroes with assembly-line speed, yet expects them to be flawless and stand the test of time, LeBron James had long ago crossed the lines from the obscure, to the familiar, to the famous. He had shown signs of being precocious beyond his years, not only as a highly honored basketball player, but as an individual who acted with the kind of maturity many of his elders never attained.

In three short professional basketball years, James had been asked to make the leap from high school phenomenon, whose secondary school years had been spotlighted like no other in the sport's history, to a franchise savior for Cleveland. Beyond that his fame and skills had almost immediately been extrapolated to serve as the new face of a National Basketball Association that had been on a wild goose chase for another Michael Jordan.

Level-headed beyond his years, James resolutely stuck to the notion that he was no second coming of Michael Jordan, but rather the first coming of LeBron James. That would have to suffice.

When he arrived in that hallway to greet gathered media before the early-season Atlanta Hawks game, James sparkled, figuratively and literally. His ensemble included a black velour jacket and diamond earrings in each ear. He listened carefully to his inquisitors and paused thoughtfully when asked a philosophical question that might have been equally appropriately posed to an athlete nearing retirement. Yet it was also the type of question that the most precocious of our athletes hear when they have made their mark but are still establishing their identity.

Many years ago, Boston Red Sox baseball star Ted Williams said early in his career that he wanted to be remembered as the best hitter who ever lived. A similar line was attributed to the Robert Redford character in the movie "The Natural" and was adjusted for James. He was asked if he had given any thought to himself in such terms as related to basketball.

"I've always just wanted to be the best player and the best person I can be at the end of my career," James said in his mini-press conference. "That's satisfying to me. I'm happy. I don't judge my career by saying I want to be better than this person or that person at the end of my career because it's not possible. The only person on and off the court to satisfy is me."[1]

And then LeBron James exited, stage right, to prepare himself to play basketball and to satisfy himself—and 20,000 spectators—with his jump shots, rebounds, and passes.

NOTE

1. LeBron James, press conference, Cleveland, Ohio, Nov. 7, 2006.

TIMELINE: EVENTS IN THE LIFE OF LEBRON JAMES

30 December 1984	Born in Akron, Ohio.
1984–1994	Impoverished James moves from home to home in Akron with single mother Gloria.
1994–1996	Moves in with Coach Frank Walker for 1½ years and improves school work.
Summer 1996	Northeast Shooting Stars win first national Amateur Athletic Union basketball championship, 12-and-under.
September 1999	James and several basketball friends from the Shooting Stars enroll at St. Vincent-St. Mary private high school in Akron.
	Emerges as a high school football star for St. Vincent-St. Mary playing the position of wide receiver.
December	Makes high school basketball debut.
March 2000	27–0 St. Vincent-St. Mary wins Ohio State Championship. James averages 18.7 points per game.
March 2001	St. Vincent-St. Mary wins second straight Ohio title game. James is named state player of the year.
February 2002	Becomes the first high school athlete who is not yet a senior to appear on the cover of *Sports Illustrated*.
March	St. Vincent-St. Mary loses Ohio state championship title game. James is chosen state player of the year for a second time.

April	Named *Parade* magazine, *USA Today*, and Gatorade high school player of the year.
June	Hurts a wrist in a summer basketball game, solidifying his resolve not to play high school football anymore because of the risk of serious injury.
December	ESPN2 televises a St. Vincent-St. Mary game nationally with high-profile basketball commentators Dick Vitale and Bill Walton.
	James's mother rewards his basketball and school accomplishments with the gift of a $50,000 Hummer, paid for with loans. The purchase leads the Ohio High School Athletic Association to investigate, but James is cleared in "Hummergate."
February 2003	The Ohio High School Athletic Association rules James ineligible for accepting sports jerseys from a store in an incident labeled "Jerseygate," but the courts limit the penalty to a two-game suspension.
March	St. Vincent-St. Mary wins its third Ohio state crown in James's four seasons. James becomes the first player to be selected state player of the year for a third time.
April	Named *Parade* magazine, *USA Today*, and Gatorade player of the year each for the second time.
May	Announces he will turn professional and make himself available for the NBA draft and signs a $90 million shoe contract with Nike.
	The hometown Cleveland Cavaliers win the draft lottery and the right to make the first selection in the annual NBA draft. The Cavs immediately announce they will choose James.
June	The Cavaliers make it official and select James with the first overall pick in the NBA draft. He signs the standard three-year NBA rookie contract with an option for a fourth year for nearly $13 million.
October	Makes his NBA debut with the Cavaliers and scores 25 points.
December	The Cavaliers are chosen to play on national TV on Christmas Day for the first time in 14 years.
March 2004	James scores career-high 41 points in a game.

April	The Cavaliers finish the regular season shy of the play-offs with a record of 35–47, but the mark represents an improvement of 18 games in the win column.
June	Named rookie of the year after averaging 20.9 points a game as an 18- and 19-year-old.
Summer	James is a member of the American bronze-medal-winning basketball team in the Summer Olympics in Athens, Greece.
6 October	Son LeBron James Jr. born to LeBron James and girl-friend Savannah Brinson.
November	Still 19, becomes the youngest player to score 2,000 points in an NBA career.
March 2005	Scores 56 points against the Toronto Raptors, his career high and the most points scored by a Cavalier player since the franchise was founded in 1970.
April	Cavaliers record winning record of 42–40 for the first time since 1998. James improves his scoring to 27.2 points a game.
December	Scores 52 points in a game against the Milwaukee Bucks.
February 2006	Named the outstanding player in the NBA All-Star game.
April	Averages 31.4 points a game and leads the Cavaliers to a 50–32 regular-season record, the team's best since 1993. The Cavs reach the playoffs for the first time since 1998 and defeat the Washington Wizards 4–2 to capture the first-round series. The Cavs lose to Detroit, 4–2, in the second round of Eastern Conference play.
Summer	Practices and competes on the United States' bronze-medal-winning team in the World Championships in China.
April 2007	The Cavaliers again win 50 games and blitz the Wizards 4–0 in the first round of the playoffs.
May	The Cavaliers topple the New Jersey Nets in the second round of the playoffs.
June	The Cavaliers upset the favored Detroit Pistons, 4–2. In the critical fifth game, James wows the nation with one of the greatest clutch solo performances in

league annals, scoring 48 points, including his squad's last 25 in a row in a double overtime triumph.

The Cavaliers advance to the NBA Finals for the first time in team history, but are swept 4–0, by the San Antonio Spurs.

15 June Bryce Maximus James, LeBron James's second child, is born.

July Co-hosts the ESPYS on national TV, the Academy Awards of sports.

August LeBron James plays for Team USA's gold-medal-winning squad in the FIBA Americas tournament that qualifies the Americans for the 2008 Summer Olympics in Beijing.

September LeBron James appears as guest host for the satirical TV show, "Saturday Night Live."

Chapter 1

BEGINNINGS

In a basketball era when so-called street scouts, Amateur Athletic Union coaches, college coaches, and professional team scouts scan the globe for talent, a prodigy jumps onto radar screens at an early age. There are scouting services that teams subscribe to heralding the next great seventh grader. By the time they are 12, the best players are singled out by age group.

Some parents and coaches consider this an unhealthy practice. The reality is that such rankings are calculated and, if a youngster is singled out, it can either spoil him or carve a path to easy street. LeBron James was nationally renowned by age 18, but he was nationally known by the cognoscenti long before that.

LeBron James was born on December 30, 1984, to Gloria James, then a 16-year-old high school student. James shares a birthday with famed golfer Tiger Woods, who is nine years older. Ronald Reagan had just won his second term in the White House and the cold war was winding down. Literary scholars were curious to discover just how much George Orwell's glum view of society, discussed in his decades-old novel *1984*, would resemble reality. In the basketball world, the Boston Celtics-Los Angeles Lakers (Larry Bird-Magic Johnson) NBA rivalry was in its heyday and Boston was the reigning champion.

The first African American Miss America, Vanessa Williams, was forced to resign after nude pictures of her appeared in *Penthouse* magazine. Under Reagan's leadership, the United States' social mores had grown more conservative. Social services programs for welfare and food stamps were in effect, but politicians made hay by belittling the lower class as slackers who didn't want to work and verbally attacking single parents as irresponsible.

None of the doings in the outside world relieved the reality of the harsh circumstances a single mother like Gloria James—raised in the same city she now sought to raise her son in—faced.

Gloria James was only a junior when she became pregnant, but she doggedly completed her high school diploma. She was also a single mother every step of the way, however, and James never knew his father. Gloria James said James's father is named Anthony McClelland, but he split up with her before the boy's birth and was never a presence in his life. There were several strikes against James's chances of becoming a success in a late twentieth-century inner-city, urban setting. He was poor, black, and fatherless.

Once Gloria James gave birth to LeBron, she was at a disadvantage both in school and society. A high percentage of unwed, teenage mothers drop out of school and only the most single-minded reach graduation. Gloria was determined to remain in school for her diploma, but the only way she and her youngster could survive financially was by relying on her mother, Freda, to house them. Freda was also a single parent then and was not flush with cash, either. The James's existence was tenuous, but Gloria's brothers and cousins contributed to LeBron's upbringing.

Mother and son lived in Akron, Ohio, merely an hour south of where James now plays for the Cleveland Cavaliers. When James was a baby, Gloria and other relatives called him "Bron-Bron," as if he was some kind of sweet treat. In a way he was. At first, James and his mom lived on Hickory Street, where Gloria grew up with her two brothers. Gloria James struggled to support her only child and they endured a life of poverty when he was a youth.

Gloria scrapped for any source of income once she left high school, but the pressures of raising a child often interfered with attempts to hold jobs long term. Whenever there was a choice to be made between spending time caring for LeBron or sticking with a job, Gloria stuck by her son. This situation became more of an issue when James was a toddler. As a single parent, Gloria James had looked to her own mother for assistance raising the baby. But James's grandmother was dying of gradually debilitating health problems, the origins of which she even kept from her daughter, and that put more stress on the boy's mother. Freda was Gloria's security blanket, the source of last resort against being forced out on the street, and now she was gone.

Gloria worked as a retail clerk in several establishments and, because she had a talent with numbers, did some rudimentary accounting work.

These were the most difficult of times for James and his mother. They moved from place to place frequently and sometimes did not know where their next meal would be eaten. James's mom was dating a local man named Eddie Jackson, who served as a surrogate father for years. Even after Gloria James and Jackson broke up, Jackson stayed in contact and remained an important male figure in James's life. He showed nothing but affection to the youngster, and LeBron has always referred to him as his most significant father figure.

James's first exposure to basketball was as a game to occupy his time, not as a sport. His mom bought him a kid's hoop with a small rubber ball for indoor play and the toddler was fascinated by it. The set was a Christmas gift as LeBron was turning 3. James seemed to take to basketball the way Einstein took to math, naturally and with great gusto. Even as a preschooler James was known to smile when he put the ball through the hoop. The object of the game seemed clear to him from the beginning. If that toy is worthy of a joyful memory, it is tempered by the timing of Freda's death at age 42. The cause of death was listed as a heart attack suffered on Christmas Eve that year. Gloria was only 19 at the time.

As a professional, James stands 6-foot-8 and weighs 240 pounds. Basketball observers have long commented on the smoothness of his moves for a man so large, and James exhibited those skills when he was a youngster and began playing organized ball for the first time. James started playing for local Akron kids' teams when Michael Jordan was at the apex of his game, leading the Chicago Bulls to six NBA titles in the 1990s. Right away, as so many other youngsters did nationwide, James tabbed Jordan as his favorite player. In James's case, that also meant requesting the number 23—same as Jordan—as he grew up. Some years later, when he could reflect on his allegiance to the Bulls' star, James said he also absorbed lessons from watching Jordan excel on the court.

"You know how a guy can make his team so much better?" James said. "That's one thing I learned from watching Michael Jordan."[1]

LIVING WITH POVERTY

Moving from apartment to apartment when the rent came due and Gloria could not make the payments did not help James find stability in his early life. Once they were even evicted from a building that was condemned and torn down. Perhaps because of these early experiences, James did not initially do well in school and he did not make friends easily. He quickly made his mark on the playing fields, however. For those who recognize James as an all-star basketball player and advertising pitch man, it may be surprising to discover that he first succeeded on the football field. By the time he was 10 years old, James's superior speed and coordination were apparent to the other children. As a fifth grader in Pee Wee football, James scored 19 touchdowns in six games.

The team's coach, Frank Walker, father of Frankie Walker Jr., one of James's best friends, took a keen interest in James. He felt the boy had great potential in the classroom, as well as in sporting endeavors. It was a particularly rough time financially for Gloria James, and when Walker offered to take her son in, care for him, and tutor him, she reluctantly allowed the arrangement. LeBron was always her pride and joy and she had worked feverishly to care for him properly, but they spent 18 months living apart. Walker's efforts helped ground James in school and advance his standing. Despite not living with Gloria for that period when he was 10 and 11 years old, James saw his mother frequently and the bond between them was never shaken. He was grateful to the Walkers for their unselfishness, but James has always called his mother his best friend.

"My mom and I have always been there for each other," James said.[2] "The Walkers will never know what a difference they made in my life."[3]

Besides his influence in football and academics, Frank Walker Sr. also introduced James to basketball as a sport as it is played in playgrounds and in gyms, not merely as an in-house baby diversionary toy.

For most of his years between ages 6 and 12 (except for the time spent with the Walkers), LeBron James and his loving mother were nomads, moving from house to house, depending on the kindness of family members or neighbors. These were tough neighborhoods where violent crime was common and poverty was ever present. There was generosity among friends, but limits to it, and Gloria and LeBron could not stay indefinitely with those who opened their small homes to help. Part of their time was spent residing in Elizabeth Park, a potentially explosive area for those looking for trouble. If he was not under the positive influence of his mother, or if he had been another type of child by nature, James could easily have become a statistic—either a corpse before his time, or a jailed youth incarcerated for law breaking. He escaped both of those fates.

"Anybody who knows about Elizabeth Park knows how bad it is," James said later. "You had gunshots flying and cop cars driving around there all the time. As a young boy it was scary, but I never got into none of that stuff. That just wasn't me. I knew it was wrong."[4]

Founded in 1825 as a shipping community on the Ohio and Erie Canal, Akron, James's hometown, is currently a city of about 217,000 people. It had made its way in the world as a manufacturing town and was proud of its nickname, "Rubber Capital of the World." Tires are a famous and popular export, the wheels that make Detroit steel roll down the road. Firestone Tire and Rubber Company was founded in 1900 and Goodyear Tire and Rubber was founded in 1898. Goodyear's corporate headquarters is still located in Akron. The American Cereal Co. and Quaker Oats also came to prominence in Akron. The firm's advertising, showing cereal shot from a cannon, registered in Americans' minds.

Somewhat in the shadow of Cleveland, Ohio's largest metropolitan area situated less than an hour north, Akron suffered as American jobs fled to lower-wage-paying Latin American countries in the 1970s and beyond. Akron's recent population reached its apex of about 290,000 in 1960, but has declined steadily since. A major feature of the city now, however, is the Polymer Science Institute of the University of Akron. The rust belt community is going high tech. Every American city has something to be proud of and every American city has neighborhoods it worries about. During LeBron's formative years, the James family was stuck in those hard-luck neighborhoods where not even the best of intentions are always enough.

Every celebrity who emerges from poverty has done so through the force of his own effort to some degree, but likely in conjunction with someone's helpful guiding hand. Sometimes only a gentle nudge is needed. Sometimes a strong presence is important. Little kindnesses or wise judgments passed on can make all of the difference. James was a first-class athlete the first time he shot baskets at a telephone pole hoop in his neighborhood. He was better than the other kids. When they played street football he outplayed them on the asphalt, catching passes and running for scores.

HELPING HANDS

Bruce Kelker spotted that talent as a volunteer coach for the Akron South Rangers Pee Wee football team and signed up James. James, who has always praised his teammates' efforts and done his best not to overshadow them, became pals with the other players. That's how he met Frankie Walker Jr. and his dad. Frank Walker Sr. was employed by the Akron Metropolitan Housing Authority. His professional background helped him relate to LeBron and Gloria. Theirs were the type of housing difficulties Walker encountered on the job all the time. The triggering event for Walker and his wife Pam to take in James for what became a year-and-a-half stay was LeBron's failure to return to school after Christmas break while in fourth grade. Walker imagined the youngster heading for a life of trouble if he didn't catch a break.

In a moment of candor during an early interview, James admitted that he and his mother often worried and were "really scared about what would happen next."[5]

Suddenly, James had three families who cared about him. His mother Gloria was in the forefront—he never doubted her love. On his adidas Pro Model basketball shoes, James later made his feelings for his mom very clear, for everyone to read. Etched in three lines are the words "Gloria Marie James." He also has "Gloria" tattooed on his biceps, mixing with other colorful upper-body tattoos. And when he talks about his mother, the grown-up James still peppers speech with references to her as his best friend. The South Rangers were a family of their own, buddies whose friendships transcended the gridiron. The Walkers, who have two children besides Frankie Jr., provided a third caring cocoon.

A youngster toted from place to place understands best what he knows and recognizes at the moment. In hindsight he better understands what was going on his life as a youth. Later, the older James grasped the gift provided by the Walkers at a vulnerable time. "It was like a new beginning for me," he said. "When I moved in with the Walkers, I went from missing 87 days my fourth-grade year to zero days in the fifth grade. They all may not know how much I care about them, but I care about them a lot. I love them."[6] But James also credits his mother for helping him regain standing by helping him over one long weekend of work with the more than 100 homework assignments he had failed to turn in.

James does not present the image of a bitter man, but he has not forgotten the hardships of his youth either. In one interview, James said that when he was five years old he remembers moving seven times. "We moved from apartment to apartment, sometimes living with friends. My mom would always say, 'Don't get too comfortable because we may not be here long.'"[7]

The Jameses were on welfare part of the time. When LeBron lived with the Walkers, Gloria saw him on weekends and gave him the only gifts she could afford—food stamps.

James dabbled in basketball from the time he received his favorite childhood toy, but he had never practiced the sport and had never learned the basics and fundamentals in an organized way. He knew the object of the game was to make baskets and score more than the other team, but he didn't have the rudiments of team play installed in him until he was 10 years old. At that time he lost a game of one-on-one to Frankie Walker Jr. The shorter player had more savvy and knew the sport. James was discouraged, but Frank Walker Sr. witnessed the defeat and promised to teach James how to play so that it wouldn't happen again.

James was a raw talent, but he lapped up instruction greedily. If he was shown a move once, he could mimic it. He had an actor's ability to pick up mannerisms and styles. The quick learning curve enhanced the natural speed, jumping ability, and quickness already on hand. James's earliest coaches also noted some of his other traits that have endured through the passage of years and the escalation of James's basketball career from youth leagues to the big leagues.

The player was ultra-competitive, but he acted maturely when he lost. He always praised his teammates' contributions—critical as time passed and it became clear that the spotlight was always going to shine its brightest on him. And James always displayed the ability to think ahead, to see ahead on the court. A major attribute of a great all-around basketball player is the ability to see the floor as a play unfolds, to anticipate what will happen when players run down-court, and to influence the outcome with a dribble, a pass, or a shot. That skill is regarded by most basketball observers as a god-given gift, one that must be bestowed from heaven more than developed on earth. The instinct so evident in the play of a Bob Cousy, Oscar Robertson, Magic Johnson, or John Stockton during succeeding eras of the NBA was part of LeBron James's package from the start.

Walker said that as a fifth grader, James was as much chess player as basketball player on the court. He knew the game so well and could show others how to approach fundamentals so easily that Walker made James an assistant coach for the fourth graders.

BECOMING THE HOOPS KING

King James—it is a flashy nickname. When it was first applied to LeBron James as a teenager by friends and local newspaper reporters, it seemed a touch premature, a tad arrogant. As if the intense attention garnered for his play on the court did not produce enough heat-lamp intensity, James acquired a lightning-rod nickname.

It is tough enough to live up to the hype, but if you fail with a moniker like King James, you invite ridicule. The pressure is there all of the time to dominate, to star, to create basketball magic. If you are unable to live up to the expectations of the masses, the next thing you know you are downgraded in print to mere prince, duke, or—horrors—even worse, a commoner. Trash talkers would have a field day if James did not play up to the name.

Yet James never shied away from either the spotlight or the focus on becoming King James. Becoming the king of his own court, of any court, came naturally to him. Even if easing into the role of royalty was as smooth as slipping into a custom-made wardrobe (something in his future), James never looked down on his loyal subjects. Instead, he always lauded his court. For that matter, James rarely thought of himself as the king who was the leader of a nation. He preferred comparing himself to the lion, the king of the jungle. That's how he saw himself, a predator on the court, the boss of the jungle-like survival battles in the low post where opponents threw elbows. He prowled through the overhanging vines and the thick trees to strike. He was that kind of lion, first and foremost. Still, there is a popular poster of James that combines the images. James is seated on a throne and surrounded by lions.

James's basketball education began under Walker in kids' ball. He was a quick study and grew quickly, too. He made friends with other players and they teamed to form a formidable summer Amateur Athletic Union (AAU) team that brought glory to Akron and renown to James.

The days when basketball, or any major American sport, was considered a seasonal hobby for high school kids are long past. If you excel at a game, scouts and coaches at a higher level want you to concentrate solely on that game. The once-commonplace three-sport high school letterman is a rarity. The old football in the fall, basketball in the winter, baseball in the spring athlete following the school calendar is an endangered species. Now even young athletes are specialists, coaxed into giving up a sport played just for fun to emphasize growth in a sport that may someday earn them a college scholarship or big money in a professional career.

Concurrently, there has been a proliferation of specialist summer camps and teams. Players may attend a camp that offers high level instruction and sunup-to-sundown play in the sport of their choice. They may also compete on touring teams that play games around their home state or in tournaments in central gathering places like Las Vegas. In no other sport has such a pattern emerged with such intensity and influence over young athletes as it has in basketball.

Players may be paired with other stars from their own state to form an all-star team. They may play many more games over the summer than are sanctioned in winter by high school governing bodies. And summer coaches may gain more influence with the players than their high school coaches, or even their parents, when it comes to decisions about where to play college ball, or if they even should forsake that opportunity for the pros.

By the time he turned 12, James was permanently reunited with his mother in a two-bedroom apartment, and he showed signs of being a gifted middle school student, recording B and B+ averages. The Jameses most difficult days were behind them. Neither could imagine the fame and fortune about to follow so soon after long years of struggle. James no longer missed classes (or days of school) in bunches and exhibited a new-found discipline with homework and assignments.

FAMILY TIES

Once Gloria James acquired the two-bedroom apartment, James's life became more stable. Her brothers, James's uncles, Terry and Curt, tried to help with his upbringing and offer some guidance. So did Eddie Jackson, Gloria's serious boyfriend. Although Jackson and Gloria ultimately split up and Jackson had brushes with the law that sometimes required terms in jail, Jackson always professed love for James, and said he would always make himself available to offer help.

Jackson said he started dating Gloria when LeBron was about eight months old and they were a couple until James was about three. Jackson remained close to the family and helped with financial matters for years afterwards.

James first competed in AAU summer basketball when he was in the fifth grade. The squad was called the Shooting Stars, and it brought together several high quality players under the mentorship of Coach Dru Joyce Jr., whose own son, Dru III, better known as Little Dru, became one of James's closest friends. Another talented player in the group was Sian Cotton. They became a sort of Three Musketeers, hanging out together, playing ball together, and spending off-court time together.

Willie McGee rounded out the group after he moved from Chicago to Akron in junior high, and the foursome became inseparable throughout high school. Romeo Travis, who the quartet played pickup games with at the Akron Jewish Community Center on Sunday nights, was another pal. A volunteer coach at the Community Center was Keith Dambrot, who had been head coach at Central Michigan University, but was temporarily out of the college game. Dambrot played a major role in the players' development and achievements later.

Although high school level coaching has morphed from a parent helping out to a teacher doing it for the extra money, to coaches who are true students of the game, few high schools could claim the services of someone as knowledgeable and sophisticated as Dambrot. He had already coached at a higher level, so he could make savvy judgments about the talent standing of James and his partners. He also had the know-how to tutor them so they could advance to play the college game.

The players were not troublemakers in any way. They stayed clean, played hard, and formed special bonds as they improved as players and gained a reputation with their success. McGee was a latecomer. He grew up in the Windy City, but he had an older brother who enrolled at the University of Akron. So McGee moved to Akron for high school and at first joined a rival summer league team. But the Shooting Stars were more advanced than McGee's team and even his own coach encouraged him to switch.

When McGee became a Shooting Star, everything clicked. He was the missing piece of the puzzle on the court and fit in just as well with the guys off the court. From elementary school through high school, the other Shooting Stars were together and became a force on the national age-group basketball scene. To advance to national competition, an AAU team must play itself out of its region and out of its state, meaning it must keep winning. The first time James and his cohorts qualified for national play they were entered in the 12-and-under age division in a tournament in Orlando, Florida in 1997. Competing against 31 other teams, the Shooting Stars captured the title. The Most Valuable Player? LeBron James. It was a harbinger of things to come. The Orlando showing was the first of six national championships won by the core group of Akron players.

Some basketball observers wonder if intensity of play at a young age is good for those just emerging from childhood. Others believe it is the only way to go for topnotch players who want to compete against the best. College and professional sports teams always say they grow closer and develop tighter friendships when spending time on the road. This was certainly true for the Shooting Stars. The road also brings its own perils—many a team has been brought down by road-trip violations or rule breaking. If the Shooting Stars had not been closely observed by Coach Joyce, and if they were not inherently well behaved, they could have found themselves in hot water.

STARDOM WITH THE SHOOTING STARS

What the Shooting Stars did over a six-year period was win basketball games and have a blast. Those two things were linked.

By showing off skills on so many stages around the country, top-shelf players become known quantities for scouting services. Players like James stand out in competition against players their own age, and the name and team are filed for future reference. When a team wins a national title at any age group, it is a magnificent achievement. If it happens just once it may be dismissed as a fluke, but when a team like the Shooting Stars appears on the scene, especially from a place like Akron, which is not regarded as a hotbed of hoops talent the way some much larger cities are, it is a statement. When it is apparent from casual observation that the team is led to championships over and over by the same star, that player takes on mythical proportions in ratings systems. The consistency of the Shooting Stars' success meant that LeBron James literally grew up in front of a wide variety of discerning hoops evaluators. It was no surprise that they labeled him the sport's "Next Great Thing."

Sometimes young talents take possession of a game and of their reputation by inundating foes with points. They score from all over the map, leaving fans oohing and aahing. James had that capability and put on shows with fresh moves and scoring eruptions wherever the Shooting Stars traveled. But he was not a ball hog. He did not force his shots as much as take them within the flow of the game. He was such an adept playmaker that he reveled in making passes that set up his teammates as much as he did while scoring. This unselfishness was a trait not often seen among superstars. Falling in love with assists as well as points when he didn't have to was something that endeared James to basketball purists. They loved him even more when they talked to Coach Joyce.

What Joyce extolled in James was his work ethic, his desire to improve, and his hunger for victory. "LeBron has those kinds of things every coach wishes they could take credit for, but you just can't," Joyce said. James, he said, always wanted to be on the court, working on his game, not running the streets. "He never missed a practice. I mean, he always wanted to be in the gym. He's always wanted to learn. The thing that kind of separates him is, everything comes so easy, and he works at it."[8]

Players most dedicated to the game, whether it is basketball, baseball, or football, demonstrate an inner drive to excel. Many times they must overcome financial limitations that prevent them from owning the finest equipment. Many do not have a father on hand who can play catch with them or teach them the finer points of a sport. They do not always even have access to a gym to practice their shooting alone. Yet such athletes make do.

When he was still learning how to play basketball, before he was even exposed to the Shooting Stars, James created his chances to shoot around on Hickory Street. A milk crate was nailed to a telephone pole and for a while that makeshift hoop—not so far removed from the style of basketball inventor James Naismith's peach basket—was his target.

NOTES

1. Mark Stewart, *Star Files*, LeBron James (Chicago: Raintree, 2006), p. 9.

2. Stewart, p. 6.

3. Stewart, p. 11.

4. David Lee Morgan Jr., *The Rise of A Star: LeBron James* (Cleveland: Gray & Company Publishers, 2003), p. 28.

5. Ryan Jones, *King James—Believe the Hype, The LeBron James Story* (New York: St. Martin's Press, 2003), p. 22.

6. Morgan, pp. 33–34.

7. B. J. Robinson, *LeBron James—King of the Court* (East Cleveland: Forest Hill Publishing, 2005), pp. 16–17.

8. Jones, p. 26.

Chapter 2

HIGH SCHOOL DAYS

By the time high school beckoned, LeBron James and his best friends from the Shooting Stars had been playing basketball together for years. They had toured the land, won major championships all over the United States, and honed their chemistry through hundreds of hours of practices and games.

The last thing that James, Joyce, Cotton, and McGee wished to do was split up the act. They did not all live in the same school district where they would naturally enroll. After some consultation, they decided they wanted to stay together and play together throughout high school. That meant they had to find a high school that would take them as a package deal.

In more innocent times, students usually attended the school where they lived. Over time, that simple approach has changed. Street agents help steer star players to high schools to play for a specific coach. Sometimes a brother or cousin could come along, too. Sometimes adults overwhelmed the player. This time the players were in charge. They wanted to stick together and by selecting a private school with no geographical boundaries, they could. LeBron James was the prize catch, but the others were also first-class players who would be welcome additions to just about any high school team.

During their Sunday night pickup games at the Akron Jewish Community Center, the players were tutored by Keith Dambrot. Dambrot had already been an NCAA Division I head coach and, among other jobs in his apprenticeship, had served as an assistant coach at the University of Akron. He had been a 32-year-old head coach at Central Michigan, labeled an up-and-comer in the profession. But then he made a terrible mistake. In the heat of a game he unprofessionally uttered a racial epithet. He had naively attempted to bond through language with black players but was roasted for his choice of words. Dambrot opened a tinderbox that brought national negative attention to him, his team, and his school. He was at first suspended and then fired by the university. Once a shooting star himself, Dambrot was living in Akron teaching basketball to the Shooting Stars in his spare time. The players who absorbed his knowledge were mostly black.

Dambrot agonized over his careless mistake and for a while it seemed he was blacklisted, untouchable, and unhirable for any basketball coaching job. He tried to obtain a public high school coaching job in Akron, but was rebuffed. Finally, Dambrot's road to resurrection began when Akron's St. Vincent-St. Mary High School hired him for the 1998–99 season. By the standards of his previous career path, he was accepting a minimum-wage, bottom-of-the-totem-pole job. But to Dambrot, after five years of working as a stockbroker, the job represented a fresh start doing the thing he loved most—coaching basketball. It is a tribute to Dambrot, LeBron James, and James's friends, that leadership he provided, coupled with the close relationships formed, provided a rehabilitation forum for Dambrot and glory for all.

Dambrot's coaching debut at St. Vincent brought the team to the regional finals—without the fab four. Then Dru Joyce III, known as Little Dru, the most involved of the four players in Dambrot's Sunday night basketball clinics, decided he wanted to play for the coach in high school. If he had stayed home, Little Dru would have played for Buchtel High, where his father was an assistant coach. In what had to be an uncomfortable conversation, he had to inform his dad he would rather play at another school.

"I just thought Coach Dambrot was a good coach and I could learn a lot of stuff from him," Little Dru said. "That all four of us could."[1]

In a sense, Little Dru had made the decision for all four friends. They were all on board. Once the players committed, Dru Joyce Jr., his father, and Lee Cotton, Sian's dad, hired on at St. Vincent as assistant coaches. This type of mass commitment, with parents coming along, too, creates hard feelings in the coaching world, and suspicion of recruitment and illegal incentives. Gossip was rampant in Akron, but no evidence of wrongdoing surfaced. Any illegal activity would have been suicide for Dambrot, who was aching for a fresh start, and would have made no sense. The boys were sincere about staying together and they found a way to make it happen.

LeBron James and his gang enrolled in the Catholic school with a student body of about 500 in the fall of 1999. Tuition was $4,800, far from a trifling for single mom Gloria James. But the school granted scholarships to worthy students and James by then had proved his prowess in the class-room. St. Vincent had a sound athletic reputation, but it was assumed that its basketball team was certain to rise in stature. Not foreseen was the impact that a 6-foot 14-year-old LeBron James would have on the football team's fortunes.

FOOTBALL

James was blessed with large hands. That physical attribute not only helped him control a basketball when dribbling, it also enabled him to pluck flying pigskins out of the air. In football parlance, he had great hands. When he ran his receiver routes, James made acrobatic catches and held onto the ball as if his fingers were coated with Super Glue. He started for the St. Vincent-St. Mary Irish his freshman year and became an all-state wide receiver as a sophomore.

Spending much time as a decoy his first season, James made a limited impact as a freshman. As a sophomore, however, he caught 42 passes for 840 yards and 11 touchdowns. Such statistics ignite interest in college recruiters. Although he was raw at football compared to basketball, it has often been suggested that James would have become a college star and might have had pro capability in that sport.

By the end of James's sophomore year of high school, he was nationally known for his basketball talent. Basketball observers began to fear that he was jeopardizing a multimillion-dollar future by playing the high-risk sport of football. Everyone knew that just one misstep, one awkward landing, or one ferocious tackle could ruin a knee. Even Gloria was edgy. Mother and son suffered through deprivation together. She had not known she was raising a prodigy whose basketball skill could forever end their economic woes. James, they were being told by basketball people in the know, had the skill to set himself up for life. Why risk that now? She hoped her son would forgo football after his sophomore year. In keeping with James's character, attitude, and outlook, however, at the last minute in the fall of his junior year he joined the team again. Protecting LeBron the only way she could, his mother took out an insurance policy that guarded against career-ending injury.

James made up his own mind about football and chose to stay a kid in an extracurricular activity rather than sideline himself and eliminate a pursuit he enjoyed. "People can say I'm stupid," James said. "But it's my decision to make and I feel it's the right one."[2]

James was better than ever that season—the key offensive weapon on the St. Vincent football team. James missed the first game of the season because he did not have the Ohio high school minimum number of practices under his belt, but in a 10–4 season that led to a regional title and concluded in a state championship semifinal game, James caught 52 passes for 1,310 yards and 15 touchdowns. Considered one of the fastest and most agile of players in the NBA today, James exhibited those traits running downfield back then. In a football-mad state, James had some coaches salivating, even if it was understood that basketball was his top priority.

The Irish's head football coach was Jay Brophy, a former member of the Miami Dolphins. An assistant coach was Mark Murphy, one-time safety with the Green Bay Packers. They both believed that James had the potential to play in the National Football League if he stuck with football.

Brophy said James's all-around competitiveness was unrivaled. "If you challenged him in racquetball and you beat him," Brophy said, "he'd be a gracious loser. He'd go practice for a week, then call you for a rematch and kick your ass."[3]

Football was a bonus. In terms of an orchestra warming up its instruments, it was the vamp-till-ready. Football was the appetizer; basketball was the main course.

FRESHMAN HOOPS

St. Vincent-St. Mary was coming off a 16–9 basketball season when James and his friends joined Dambrot and a roster with some carryover talent. The Irish roster was loaded with good players, but in James Dambrot inherited an exceptional talent. James stood 6-foot-4 for his freshman basketball season and weighed a still slender 170 pounds. It has often been noted that James looks much older than his years, but in pictures taken during his first two years of high school he looks very much the teenager still growing into manhood and into his body.

Dambrot's basketball instincts kicked in and he almost immediately realized that James was more than good. He told his old coaching friend Ben Braun, now the head man at the University of California at Berkeley, about James, summing up his glowing report by noting, "This guy is going to be the best guy I've ever seen." When Braun saw James play in person he promptly told Dambrot James was too good to ever play in college and that he would go directly to the NBA.[4]

James's freshman year began with a game against Cuyahoga Falls. He scored 15 points in his debut and the Irish won. In December of the 1999–2000 season, James scored a season high of 27 points. He also recorded a high school career low of 8 points in January of that season, the only time in his four-year prep career that James failed to score in double digits. James averaged more than 18 points per game as a freshman.

James demonstrated his flair for spectacular shots and for making the timely pass. Dambrot became most impressed with James's on-court cool and his decision making. "I knew he was really good when we got him off the football field," the coach said, "and he started practicing with us and I saw how smart he was."[5]

The Irish took a 20–0 record into the Ohio postseason playoffs and worked their way to the finals. In between, a deeply affected Dambrot lost his mother to cancer. Exhausted and distracted, he spent nights with her in Hospice care, worrying that he wasn't fulfilling his obligation to his players. Emotionally on edge, the players, who also liked Dambrot's mother, advanced to the championship game at Ohio State University's Value City Arena.

This was far from a one-man team. James led St. Vincent with 25 points, 9 rebounds, and 4 assists, the type of across-the-board statistical line for which he became famous. His buddy, Little Dru Joyce, scored 21 points by making seven 3-point field goals. Senior center Maverick Carter, a future college player, was actually chosen the *Cleveland Plain Dealer's* player-of-the-year. There were kudos and trophies for all when the Irish defeated Jamestown Greenview High, 73–55, to finish 27–0. Still a freshman, James was selected as the playoffs' Most Valuable Player and he was chosen first-team all-state.

Although the press built James up as a basketball prodigy, Gloria James kept telling reporters that LeBron was still a typical teenager and she had to get after him to make his bed. She also told reporters how endearing it was when he pasted up handmade Mother's Day cards for her. King James was all of 15 years old.

Despite the growth in attention, the clamoring for interviews, and the comments of scouts, as James matured on the basketball court, he insisted that he was more of a normal kid than most people thought. He told sportswriters that he liked to hang out with his friends, watch movies, and participate in all the regular high school activities.

James freely discussed his mother's influence and how they had battled through hard times together, but he never talked about girls. During high school, while being a regular guy at school dances and pep rallies, James did meet an Akron girl named Savannah Brinson. She became his steady.

From the beginning, Brinson maintained the lowest of low profiles, never appearing at press conferences either in high school or during other developments in James's career, such as his decision to go pro, or to sign with a shoe company. James and Brinson as a couple stayed out of the limelight. It was as if he had compartmentalized sections of his life, one being for fans, the other being for family.

Ultimately, as years passed, and James and Brinson stayed together, she made very brief appearances in public. Only after James became a pro was Brinson sometimes seen in public at his side, or in the family section at Cleveland Cavaliers games. Periodically, a photograph appears of the two-some on a celebrity Web site, but Brinson does not show up in entertainment publications answering 20 questions about LeBron.

Virtually the only time Brinson was in the public eye with any regularity was when she was about to give birth to the couple's children. And even then, James did all the talking. The always visible James has done a masterful job of keeping his private life private. Only once did the James–Brinson relationship make waves. In 2007, sportswriters and gossip reporters were surprised to hear their voice mail boxes fill up with venom from strangers who said they should be chastising James "the role model" for having children out of wedlock and not marrying his sweetheart.[6]

It was rare public backlash against the popular athlete, although James shrugged off the criticism. If he and Brinson had plans to wed, they kept it to themselves. But as high schoolers none of that could be anticipated and it all lay in the future.

SECOND TIME AROUND

LeBron James had arrived. Sophomore slump? Not likely. The St. Vincent-St. Mary Fighting Irish bench was not as deep as it had been during James's freshman year, but the freshmen players were now immeasurably more mature, not only from succeeding at the state championship level, but because they once again stayed together to play another AAU summer ball season. Playing 27 games together at the high school level was one thing, but the fabulous foursome had played hundreds of games together spread over a period of years. They learned and improved on the job.

James also got a chance to show his stuff on the road, spending a small portion of the summer at the Slam N' Jam camp in Oakland for a team known as Soldiers I. Chris Dennis, operator of Akron's most prominent summer tournament, made it his mission to promote James. Dennis placed James in California and then tripled his efforts to make James a known commodity to basketball shoe manufacturers, their representatives, and summer camp planners. Although the Nikes, adidas, and Reeboks of the world were not yet clamoring to convince James to join their star-studded lineups, their early exposure to him laid the foundation for a future sneakers war.

The touting of LeBron paid dividends. During the summer after his freshman year, James was invited to participate in Howard Garfinkel's famous Five-Star basketball camp. The five-day event involved instruction and pickup games and served as a showcase for up-and-coming stars. The list of future luminaries who passed through as campers read like a basketball all-star roster and included Michael Jordan, Stephon Marbury, Grant Hill, Christian Laettner, and Rasheed Wallace. All of them had been college stars and successful professionals.

James and his cohorts worked for years to put Akron basketball on the map as they piled up age-group championships. But James did as much for the city's hoops reputation—and his own—as all of his contemporaries and predecessors combined during a week in Pittsburgh. The camp was generally divided between upperclass juniors and seniors and underclass sophomores like James. James was so good that he split his time between his own age group and the older players when roster spots opened as a result of injury.

He totally dominated. When the camp ended, James was selected for the all-star team of his own division and the older division. It was an unprecedented achievement and it announced to the basketball world that young LeBron was the real deal. Between his freshman year enrollment at St. Vincent and the start of his junior year in high school, James had gone from a player known only to the best-informed followers of high school ball to a hometown hero revered throughout Ohio, and he had begun registering on name recognition charts throughout the sports world.

Athlon, for years the publisher of preseason football and basketball annuals, rated James as the top high school sophomore in the country. The *Sporting News* ranked him second. There were no secrets left in the sport. If you played in the mountains, the desert, in the snow of Alaska, on the beaches of Hawaii, in the swamps of Mississippi, scouts found you. Similarly, if college coaches saw your name on any kind of ranked ability list, they were likely to become pen pals. Just in case you had any interest at all in matriculating at their campus, they didn't want to make the mistake of overlooking you and make you think you would not be welcome.

GOING NATIONAL

James received hundreds of pieces of recruiting mail. "Dear LeBron, we love you, come to our school. We have a spot for you at Hoboken State Technical School, if you want it." That was the general thrust of the mail. When you are a 15-year-old boy, and only recently escaped from a life of poverty, that kind of overwhelming flattery can spin your head. And that's even if you have no intention of ever setting foot on the campus of an obscure school in New Mexico. The mail at least showed James that coaches knew about him and respected what he had done. But he had two more years to pad his resume, and in an age when high school athletes were making the jump directly to the pro ranks, there was no guarantee that James would be enticed into playing college basketball for a minute even at a traditional power like North Carolina, Duke, or Indiana.

The buzz about James and the St. Vincent basketball team spread far beyond the borders of the high school's campus. School officials examined the publicity evidence and made a bold business call. Instead of confining home games to the small, on-campus gym, they rented the Rhodes Arena, the 5,900-plus seat basketball building that hosted University of Akron games. St. Vincent had become a regionally popular team. Spectators wanted to see the Irish and star LeBron James in the flesh, not just read about them in the newspapers. Fans were not going to show up on the doorstep—at least not yet—from Florida, Texas or New York, but plenty of high school hoops fans from Ohio were just an hour away.

Showing an understanding that they also had a special product with James gracing the court, Dambrot and school officials scheduled six games against teams from other states. Older fans who think back to their own school days are surprised to hear this, but high school teams routinely have been taking special trips, especially over holiday vacation times like Thanksgiving and Christmas, for well over a decade. Sometimes the games are one-time showdowns featuring two teams highly rated by USA Today, the national newspaper that publishes high school rankings. Sometimes the games pit private powerhouse schools that are not subject to the same travel restrictions as public schools governed by state boards. And sometimes a school is sought because it features a once-in-a-lifetime player who single handedly temporarily raises the reputation of his team.

The defining moment of James's sophomore season came in a game against Oak Hill of Virginia. The Irish were coming off a 27–0 season and started the next campaign 9–0. James and his buddies were 36–0 [7] over two seasons when they faced Oak Hill in mid-January of 2000 in Columbus, Ohio. Oak Hill had finished 30–2 the year before and was 17–0 in the new season and ranked No. 1. Oak Hill also featured future NBA player DeSagana Diop, a 7-foot center, and other players destined for high-caliber NCAA Division I programs.

James, who had grown to 6-foot-6 by his sophomore season, scored 35 points in the game, but St. Vincent lost, 79–78. Technically, it was a neutral court game, but the fans favored the Irish. In defeat, James gained more luster. No one could question whether he was piling up statistics against middling opponents. He had played his best against the best. Future Kentucky player Rashad Carruth, one of Oak Hill's stars, called James "the best I've ever played against." And James said his ability to perform at such a high level under pressure against such a fine team gave him more confidence. "The way I played that game, it just felt like, 'Can't nobody stop me,'" he said.[7]

Sometimes when a young athlete talks brashly like that he is considered arrogant. James's forthright, but wry delivery—coupled with the fact that everyone recognized the statement as the truth—generally kept criticism to a minimum when he spoke out strongly.

Despite the loss, St. Vincent was possibly better than in James's first year. The close foursome had become a quintet. Romeo Travis, another accomplished player, transferred to St. Vincent and after an uneasy start became pals with the core of the team and a major contributor.

The Oak Hill game represented St. Vincent's only loss during the regular season. The Irish were 19–1 when the state playoffs began and, for the second year in a row, they blitzed the best of the rest of Ohio competition. The Irish won, 63–53, over Casstown Miami East in the championship game, and this time Value City Arena was sold out with about 18,000 screaming fans. The increase of nearly 5,000 fans for the title game paralleled the increase in St. Vincent's national profile.

James exulted when St. Vincent won again, proud of putting a second straight Ohio title on the team's resume.

Again showing that he was more than just a scorer, James compiled averages of 25.2 points, 7.2 rebounds, 5.8 assists, and 3.8 steals per game. James could knock 'em dead by putting the ball in the hoop, disrupting opponents defensively, collecting the ball off the glass, or by simply finding his open teammates who took advantage any time another team was reckless enough to double- or triple-team him. James was the first sophomore chosen Ohio player of the year and the first sophomore chosen as a first-team All-American by USA Today. The Sporting News tabbed James the national sophomore of the year.

There was no more fervent or visible LeBron James rooter in the stands than his mother. Because she stood barely more than 5-foot-5, it is possible that fans would not otherwise recognize her, but Gloria James regularly wore a "LeBron's Mom" T-shirt. Sometimes she draped his letter jacket over it. She always appreciated it when a journalist commented on James's good manners.

Writer B. J. Robinson described James as more than the All-American player on the court, but as more or less the All-American boy, too, who worked overtime to get his teammates involved in play. "Who wouldn't want such a player on their team?"[8]

Accolades poured in. James and his team had reached the summit of the mountain in the playoffs twice. The attention, the praise, and the evaluations of James's talent were usually reserved for seniors. He had just completed his sophomore year. James and the Irish had two more years together. They were definitely planning to win four straight Ohio high school basketball titles. None of them expected much of a change—only more of the same and better—for their junior year.

EXIT COACH DAMBROT

Little remains static in the sports world. Players graduate. Players get injured. Coaches depart. Never is one season the same as another. The upheaval that faced St. Vincent after James's sophomore year was unexpected. Coach Keith Dambrot made the most of his second chance. In his three seasons at the helm, he won about 90 percent of his games and led the school to two consecutive championships. Long ago he had been on the fast track in college basketball. Now Dambrot was redeemed, and the same college basketball world that had turned him into a virtual nonperson eight years earlier came calling. It was not a long distance call, either. Watching St. Vincent-St. Mary progress closely from a few hills over (and sometimes in their own building) officials at the University of Akron in need of a new head coach dialed Dambrot's number.

In the summer after James's sophomore year, Dambrot announced he was leaving St. Vincent to return to college. He said the players were grumpy about his decision, although they later told him they understood.

Dambrot departed with the most lavish praise for James, comparing various facets of his game with superstars Magic Johnson, Kobe Bryant, and Tracy McGrady. Dambrot knew that James was on his way to the pros and that he would not be coaching him again unless he could fast-talk him into attending the University of Akron for a year for old time's sake. The odds of that occurring were worse than the chances of breaking the bank at a major Las Vegas casino.

NOTES

1. Ryan Jones, *King James: Believe the Hype—The LeBron James Story* (New York: St. Martin's Press, 2003), p. 31.

2. David Lee Morgan Jr., *The Rise of A Star—LeBron James* (Cleveland: Gray & Company Publishers, 2003), p. 84.

3. Morgan, p. 85.

4. Morgan, pp. 60–61.

5. Jones, p. 35.

6. Connie Schultz, philly.com, June 19, 2007.

7. Jones, p. 55.

8. B. J. Robinson, *LeBron James—King of the Court* (East Cleveland: Forest Hill Publishing, 2005), p. 34.

Chapter 3

BEYOND HIS YEARS

By the time LeBron James was a junior at St. Vincent-St. Mary High School, he was as well known to basketball aficionados as Meryl Streep is to the Academy of Motion Picture Sciences. And in a way he had won his own Oscar, too.

Although the phrases that have come to describe future basketball stars such as "The Next Great Thing" or "The Next Michael Jordan" have been almost automatically applied to young men on their way up, by the time he celebrated his 17th birthday, James had become the most highly publicized high school junior in history.

Michael Jordan was not MICHAEL JORDAN until he scored the winning basket to give North Carolina an NCAA title. Kobe Bryant was not KOBE BRYANT, or "the next Michael Jordan," until after he moved directly from high school to the Los Angeles Lakers and put in a couple of hard-work seasons. James's reputation preceded him in basketball hotbeds before he came close to finishing high school.

Probably the most "normal" thing that happened in LeBron James's life during his junior year in high school was breaking a finger while playing football. It was a relatively minor injury, but it served a major purpose. All along his mother and other well-meaning friends lectured James about risking serious injury while playing football for fun when by doing so he could be throwing away a magnificent basketball career. The injury made an impression on James, and he decided he had too much at stake to continue in the sport. He never played organized football again after his junior season.

Given the way the rest of James's high school days played out, it would have been difficult to make time to play football. James had almost no privacy; he was sought after constantly for interviews. His play was scrutinized by coaches and scouts. Any move either he or his mother made that would go unremarked-upon involving another athlete was critiqued. Still, James exhibited grace under pressure. He may have felt the object of prying eyes and the object of attention by those who had no business with his business, but he either shrugged things off and remained affable, or directly dealt with sports writers' observations.

At St. Vincent, Dru Joyce II was promoted from assistant coach to take over from Dambrot. This change involved little adjustment by James or the other players, for Coach Dru had already been Coach Dru to them, not only at school, but over a stretch of several summers. The showing the Irish made in their Ohio state tournaments against Oak Hill Academy and other big-city teams meant that the team was in more demand to play big-name schools nationwide.

THE HYPE TAKES OFF

It is one thing to be noticed, quite another to be hyped. By his junior year, James was a staple of sports page stories in Akron and vicinity. He had also been written up in *SLAM*, a basketball magazine that approaches its subject matter with a more hip style than mainstream media. That *SLAM* featured James so early in his high school career anointed him as cutting edge.

There was still one way to trump *SLAM*, however. There are ways to measure that you have really made it in the United States, and when it comes to the sports world nothing is more impressive than being a cover topic for *Sports Illustrated*. *Sports Illustrated* is the most respected print medium in the sports writing field, and being featured on the cover is for many athletes a once-in-a-career pleasure. For the older sports fan who might never read a copy of *SLAM*, it is also a sign that the athlete is pretty special. In the case of someone as young as James, it was also advance advertising. *Sports Illustrated* told its few million readers that this was a fresh face to be reckoned with.

High school athletes had periodically been exposed to the masses on the cover of *Sports Illustrated* since the magazine's debut in 1954, but all of them were seniors. When James was introduced to America at large on the *Sports Illustrated* cover for the February 18, 2002 issue, he was the first high school junior to make it. James wore a green St. Vincent basketball jersey with the team's "Irish" script on the front and a headband, something that has since become a well-known trademark. In case anybody was silly enough to miss any allusions to Michael Jordan, further examination of the picture reminded them that James also wore No. 23. As if the fact that

James was on the cover, rather than simply being discussed in an inside story, did not sufficiently support the idea that *Sports Illustrated* was going whole-hog in predicting a brilliant future, the succinct, but direct, cover headline made that clear. It read: "The Chosen One."

James's background was duly reported, but the story also quoted several basketball experts with NBA know-how who could barely contain themselves in analyzing James's place in the basketball firmament. Reviewing the piece let the previously unsuspecting reader in on a secret—if James was available right then and there, NBA teams would fight and claw to sign him. All of this fuss was being made over a junior in high school, and the only reaction plausible for the sports fan that had been previously unfamiliar with Ohio high school hoops was: Holy moley.

The *Sports Illustrated* splash ratcheted up the attention—and the pressure—on James and his team. They became targets. Opposing teams used the article as a psych measure for motivation. If they contained James and beat the Irish, they knew they would gather extra attention. James, Joyce, Cotton, Travis, and McGee were too good to be threatened by most teams. In games that might be closer, however, the extra incentive couldn't hurt. Foes that were outclassed in basic skills sometimes resorted to more physical play. James was faster and taller and could out-jump most of the high school players he faced, but they all owned elbows. They could jab him, poke him, and try to slow him down. If physicality didn't work, they could at least irk him verbally to try to throw him off his game.

Gloria James sometimes grew apoplectic at what seemed to be the uncalled for hammering of her baby. In one game against George Junior Republic in Pittsburgh shortly after the *Sports Illustrated* story appeared on newsstands, she ran out on the court yelling about the treatment of James. James, who did not lose his cool, gently guided her back to her bleacher seat. Incidents like that played poorly with a skeptical media that did not know the whole story of Gloria's life with her son, how she loved him and how she had sacrificed for him. She was sometimes portrayed negatively as a stage mother. Hard-nosed strategy worked that day—St. Vincent lost, 58–57, in overtime.

It would have been easy for James to blow up in such situations, but there is no account suggesting he ever did. James never seemed particularly bothered if opposing fans ragged on him. He maintained his equilibrium, never mouthing off to them, or retaliating with negative gestures. He just ignored the clamor around him.

Attention on James and St. Vincent never receded. More and more reporters clamored for interviews. The team's locker room became off limits, much like for major college programs, and James greeted the media in press conferences seated at a table rather than by his locker, a foreshadowing of his pre-game future pattern with the Cavaliers. So many people wanted a piece of him.

"He has no life now," Coach Dru Joyce II said of James's situation. "Fame has its price. If grown men have trouble dealing with it, how do you prepare a kid for it?"[1]

Coach Joyce repeatedly told reporters that James had a supernatural maturity and a built-in sense of how to cope with the crazy level of attention.

Autograph collecting inhabited a different sphere in the sports memorabilia subculture in the 2000s than it did in 1960s America. For decades, obtaining autographs was an activity for young sports fans waiting outside the gates of a stadium, darting down to the railing at a baseball park, or shouting out a player's name. Kids handed over notebooks, scraps of paper, or collector cards and cherished the signed sheets they received for a while, before they grew up, became distracted by girls, and lost them or tossed them. No more. Autograph hunting is big business. Adults are much more engaged. More often the signature is prized for the price it can fetch at auction or at a sports collector's show than for the feel-good way it was obtained. Youngsters are raised to be discerning, to go after big stars and save the booty for later sale, perhaps to finance their college educations. It is rare indeed to come across the true-blue innocent collector seeking something to be signed simply for the thrill of interacting with a sports hero.

James had always been obliging, scrawling his autograph for anyone who asked. But the lines hadn't been long, nor the demands intense. Once the *Sports Illustrated* cover story appeared, he was besieged. And if James was an innocent, thinking everyone who lusted after his signature did it because they liked him, that innocence was quickly lost. He watched from a distance as adults sent small children with little knowledge of who he was to obtain autographs on their magazines. He saw through their ploys.

"Everybody comes up to me," James said, "all these grown folks, asking for autographs talking about it's for their kids, next thing you know, they're selling it on eBay."[2]

MAKING NEW FRIENDS THROUGH BASKETBALL

The frenzy over James and the basketball squad challenged the school administration. There were about 490 students who did not play basketball and who were trying to get an education, and the members of the boys' basketball team were fighting through their extracurricular lives to obtain a diploma, too. Demands on the team became so great and distractions so frequent that the school banned all media from the premises until after 3 p.m., when classes were out. The average citizen sometimes claims that celebrities get special treatment. It is often true in ways they do not suspect. James needed protection. He was too "special" to be left to his own devices, for he would be mobbed by admirers and diverted from actually being able to graduate from high school.

Doors closed to others do open to the gifted, however. In 2001, during the summer leading up to his junior year, James was invited to attend informal workouts at Hoops The Gym, the Chicago basketball haven where Michael Jordan trained and legendary pickup games involving him and other pros were conducted out of public view. At the time, Jordan was working in the front office of the Washington Wizards. But it was apparent to Jordan watchers that the gathering was all about getting Jordan into shape for another shot at the NBA. Among those joining James in games were Charles Barkley, Antoine Walker, Michael Finley, Juwan Howard, and Penny Hardaway.

This was fast company for a high school junior. By then James was writing a regular diary for *SLAM* and discussed the experience. "It was cool," he said. "I got to run with a lot of the other NBA guys, and I talked to Jordan a little bit."[3]

These were not the consorts of the typical high school player. Later, there would be allegations that James must have done something illegal by working out with those players that negated his amateur standing since he was still talking about his favorite colleges. Those schools included Florida, Duke, North Carolina, Michigan State, Ohio State, Cincinnati, and the University of California. The precedent of heading right from high school into the NBA draft had been well established, but James at least gave those college coaches hope. Even he was startled, though, when people openly talked of James seeking to breach NBA rules that forbade a high school player whose class had not yet graduated from entering the league.

The coming out parties in different forums such as practicing with pros were shelved in time for James to play basketball his junior year. Stories about LeBron James were no longer rudimentary, explaining that there was this guy in Akron who could be something terrific. Analysis had progressed far beyond that, raising the issue of just which former NBA star James compared most favorably with. Was it Magic Johnson? Was it Kobe Bryant? Was it Tracy McGrady, the Houston Rockets star? James never exhibited a swelled head over being named in such fine company, but he did say he was pleased to be mentioned.

"I work so hard to be noticed as the next Kobe or T-Mac," James said. "And I'm going to keep working hard so that one day they say, 'This player reminds me of LeBron James.'"[4]

JUNIOR YEAR ADVENTURES

On one level it was deemed ludicrous for LeBron James to be listed as a professional basketball prospect before finishing high school. On another level it seemed the perfect progression along the road of basketball insanity where elementary schoolchildren and junior high players were being ranked.

The National Basketball Association used to forbid teams from drafting any player whose college class had not graduated. It was a way to keep peace with the NCAA, the governing body of college sports. Similarly, other professional sports leagues had their long-established practices in the distribution of young talent. The closest parallel to the NBA was the National Football League, which also had rules in place banning the drafting of players while they were still in college.

Over time, however, the basketball rules loosened. Using the argument that the United States is a free country and that players should be allowed to pursue their vocation without restriction, basketball players challenged the rules in courts.

Spencer Haywood, an immensely talented 6-foot-8 sophomore forward at the University of Detroit, felt he was good enough to play in the NBA immediately and should not have to wait until his college class graduated. Haywood took the league to court in 1970 and the legal judgment led to exceptions in the NBA policy.

The NBA created a "hardship" clause that enabled financially challenged players who were not finished with college to declare for the draft. Eventually, all such limitations were tossed out and players coming directly out of high school became free to declare their interest and eligibility for professional ball. That rule was in effect as James was completing high school. A subsequent regulation, however, was approved through the NBA's collective bargaining agreement between players and owners, raising the minimum age for new players to 20.

No player had ever attempted to try to turn professional in the NBA before his high school class graduated—it was already frowned upon in many quarters that 18-year-olds were draft eligible. Experts said, however, that LeBron James was so good by his junior year he was capable of playing in the league immediately. Boston Celtics general manager Danny Ainge, quoted in the *Sports Illustrated* article, suggested there were only a handful of active NBA players that he wouldn't trade for James right then and there. James and his mother put the kibosh on any wild rumors he might come out. To reach an exalted status to even be discussed in such a context meant James produced a spectacular junior year of basketball achievement.

GOING PRO EXTRA EARLY?

One thing that seemed to be overlooked by those making clinical analyses of whether James had the goods to go pro as a 17-year-old was his personality. Yes, he took basketball seriously and felt his future lay in the game. But part of him also wanted to stay a kid for as long as he could. "I love high school," he said. "You can go back to college, but you can't go back to high school."[5]

Once again, St. Vincent-St. Mary would play home games at the University of Akron's gym. It was the only practical solution, as there was more demand than ever from the casual fan not affiliated with the school hoping to capture a glimpse of James and his cohorts on the court. There were also more teams than ever from other parts of the country interested in match-ups for the 2001–02 season. The Fighting Irish had become one of the teams *USA Today* considered in its national rankings. At the beginning of James's junior year, the Irish were rated No. 6 nationally by the national newspaper.

St. Vincent won the first game of James's third varsity season by a score of 81–40 over Avon Lake, another Ohio school, and that was after only one full week's worth of practice with the entire team present since the football season ran deep into the playoffs. St. Vincent plunged into serious competition in its second basketball game, facing *USA Today*'s No. 5 ranked team, Germantown Academy of Pennsylvania, and winning 70–64. James made an impression with 38 points.

This was the Irish's first season under Dru Joyce II, but there really wasn't much adjustment period for the new coach. Joyce was thrust into the white hot spotlight. More and more media members wanted a piece of LeBron James and more and more fans expected mythical performances. There was a danger between the written hype and the verbal descriptions that James was coming to be seen as superhuman. Joyce sensed this, perhaps as quickly as James.

It was after the Germantown victory that Joyce thoughtfully said out loud what only a few close James observers had whispered—the public was demanding more and more from LeBron shows.

St. Vincent had become a national touring team as much as an Ohio team. The Irish mopped up on Buckeye state opposition and survived tense challenges from other top teams across the country for a 6–0 start before competing in a Christmas tournament in Delaware.

James routinely scored 25 or 30 points in a game without forcing shots. St. Vincent had balance and other talented players. Although everyone knew James was the superstar, he was always generous on the court. A superb passer, he collected assists by feeding his teammates. In close games, when foes were better than advertised, or good enough to keep the score close, the Irish naturally looked to James to lead them and score the decisive points. He had the gift of being able to turn up his play a notch and make something happen when his team was threatened. Frank Lupica, the coach of the Walsh Jesuit Warriors Ohio team, said all James's teammates had to do was "dial 1–800-LeBron" and he rode to the rescue.[6]

Some top high school scorers never develop a complete floor game. What distinguished James was that he innately possessed the all-around instincts of a more experienced player. He knew that sometimes circumstances meant he could help his team with passes instead of shots.

St. Vincent-St. Mary beat teams from New Jersey, Michigan, Kentucky, Missouri, and Ohio. Wherever the schedule led the Irish, they came, they saw, they conquered. The Irish, however, did lose by a single point to Amityville High School from Long Island, in the Delaware Slam Dunk to the Beach Tournament, even though James scored 39 points while suffering from an illness.

Every once in a while, an interview was given by some NBA expert who couldn't stop gushing over James's potential, occasionally casually throwing in that James would be the first choice in the entire pro draft if he left high school. James reiterated that he wasn't going anywhere except St. Vincent-St. Mary the next year. The 2002 NBA draft came and went and Yao Ming, the 7-foot-6 Chinese phenom, was the No. 1 player selected. Ming turned out to be a fine choice for the Houston Rockets as he blossomed into an all-star center and helped the league develop new marketing opportunities in the world's most populous country.

NBA observers (usually anonymously) could make fantastic comments about James and not blush because of the combination of his physical and mental maturity. Not only did James seem poised in interviews, not only did he seem to have fun on the court while playing unselfishly, but he had grown to 6-foot-8 and 240 pounds. He was a teenager in a man's body and all evidence indicated he knew how to use his size. Even James, though, was mindful of the millions of eyes of the world on him that left him little escape from public inspection. In one interview with a sports Web site, James was quoted as saying, "Sometimes it feels like I have the whole world on my shoulders. I know I'm under a microscope with everything I do."[7]

James couldn't afford a misstep. He had a solid support system between his mother, coaches, teammates, and other friends. They wanted to protect him from the glare of publicity at the same time they wanted him to enjoy the liberating ride. By the nature of his expanding reputation and occasions like the off-season workout in Chicago, basketball stars took an interest in James. Antoine Walker, who had been an All-American at Kentucky and an all-star in the NBA with the Boston Celtics before he eventually won a world championship ring with the Miami Heat, was on James's speed-dial, just to offer life advice. Walker hoped to impart some of the wisdom he had gained in the sport to smooth the young man's entry into the big time. James had always been fundamentally sound on the court. People like Walker were attempting to ensure that he remained fundamentally sound off the court.

In February of James's junior year, St. Vincent journeyed to Trenton, New Jersey, for another tournament. Waiting was old nemesis Oak Hill Academy of Virginia. Not only was Oak Hill as powerful as ever, the team featured another soon-to-be household name—Carmelo Anthony. It was a wild game, a shootout par excellence between two phenomenal young players. Anthony, who attended college for one season and led Syracuse to the NCAA title as a freshman, before turning pro with the Denver Nuggets, scored 34 points. James scored 36 points, but Oak Hill prevailed, 76–66.[8]

The game partially overlapped the nearby NBA All-Star game, which was being held in Philadelphia, and the release of the famous *Sports Illustrated* issue. Kobe Bryant, the Lakers star who had gone from high school to the pros, asked what it would have been like if his picture appeared on the cover of *Sports Illustrated* when he was a junior. "As a junior?" he repeated. "I never would have gone to class."[9] Bryant noted he was joking, but it was an indicator of the temptation for an athlete to become swellheaded. James never showed that tendency. He went to class and there are no accounts of fellow students referring to him as too big for his britches, regardless of how large they were.

The schedule was more difficult and demands on the group of high school players more intense, but St. Vincent-St. Mary lost three games during the regular season of James's junior year. The Irish were still undefeated in Ohio and ranked No. 1 in the state going into the state tournament. St. Vincent was a two-time consecutive state champion and expected to win a third straight time.

James seemed philosophical in admitting that not everybody was rooting for the Irish. "Everybody wants to see the giants fall, I guess."[10] It was unclear how that opinion jibed with the belief that thousands upon thousands of fans turned out around the country to see James do fabulous things on the basketball court. But that is how he saw it.

The Irish won their regional opener by 60 points. In the second game, rather recklessly if a team was trying not to motivate James and Company, Hoban came out for warm-ups wearing "The Chosen One" T-shirts, making fun of James's *Sports Illustrated* cover. St. Vincent won by 39 points. The Irish won its quarterfinal game by 5 points and its semifinal by 29 points. The same decisive results were posted in the regional final and in the state tournament, leaving St. Vincent one win from a three-peat.

UPSET AT STATE

James, always confident, but usually more circumspect, mimicked Joe Namath who had issued his bold prediction that the New York Jets would knock off the favored Baltimore Colts to win Super Bowl III. Like Namath, James promised victory.

In a stunning upset, despite James's 32 points, the Irish lost to Roger Bacon of Cincinnati, 71–63, a team that had played them closely during the regular season. When the game ended in disappointment, James graciously proclaimed his respect and admiration for Roger Bacon's achievement. He did not hide from questions and he did not sulk.

"I'm a little bit upset with myself because I guaranteed a victory," James said. He said the loss would motivate him more for his senior year when he hoped to be the top player in America and see St. Vincent ranked Number 1 nationally as well.[11]

For the first time in their high school careers, the globetrotting Irish lost to an Ohio team; and for the first time in their high school careers, LeBron James, Dru Joyce III, Romeo Travis, and the others ended a season without a new state championship banner to hang in their gym.

Later, James blamed himself for the loss. "That was on me as a leader," he said.[12] It was a mature response, but the final loss in a 23–4 season was probably more attributable to overall team fatigue and the pressure on the team to always be up for every fan and opponent. And then there was the simple fact that in team sports competition, the end is not scripted like a Broadway play, and the underdog sometimes does win.

MORE EXCITEMENT

LeBron James may only have been entering his senior year in high school at St. Vincent-St. Mary, but he had already entered the world of celebrityhood. That curious American status wrenches a person's life from his own grasp and propels him into the realm of public property. It can be a joy ride at best, but it can be humbling and gossipy at worst. Anyone anointed by the hype machine as worthy of celebrity attention is going to have to accept the bad if he appreciates the good. There is a bizarreness associated with being unable to walk down the street unrecognized. It is unnatural to be mobbed at all times, to be begged for autographs or just "a moment of your time" incessantly. Often escaping into a cocoon of friends and relatives, such an adored person can become removed from reality. Such an admired person can become so important in his own mind that he acts selfishly not out of malice, but because his world has shrunk.

Many Americans will do just about anything to be viewed as celebrities, if only for a moment. That wish explains the popularity of so many reality television shows. Most Americans believe that any tradeoff in loss of privacy would be worth the fawning of the multitudes. Many celebrities have been too immature to handle the role, however. It takes a grounded person to skate through the firestorm of attention, to make it all work for him rather than let it overwhelm him. The pressures are intense on anyone, but especially on someone as young as LeBron James when his name was promoted to a place of honor in the basketball and sports world.

After problems early in his public school career when he and mother Gloria were moving from home to home, James became a solid student. He also sought normalcy in high school when he was walking the halls or removed from basketball. He attended school dances, he dressed up for pajama day, and he described school hours at St. Vincent between 8 a.m. and 3 p.m. as his "comfort zone." "A lot of people say high school was hard, but for me it was easy," James said. "When you have friends and people there with you that you love, it makes it a lot easier."[13] The school administrators who were accused of exploiting James because they moved games to the Akron arena and allowed some of his games to be televised worked hard to protect James from intrusions during school hours.

As he embarked on another summer tour showing off his skills for basketball fans around the country, James faced a number of risks. He could let his celebrity stature change him and take over his life, removing him figuratively, if not literally, from his teammates. He could be carelessly wooed by dollar-bill waving agents into accepting cash payments and losing the rest of his high school eligibility. Or on a rough-and-tumble play on the court, James could be injured and perhaps jeopardize his entire basketball future.

There is no evidence that James ever let his growing fame change his personality or serve as a wedge between him and his teammates. There is no evidence he succumbed to any type of illegal financial inducements bestowed on him because of his basketball talent (although there was some dispute about this). But during an early off-season game in Chicago, bad luck did arrive for James in the way of unanticipated injury.

FAME FOLLOWS ON THE ROAD

In early June the summer after his junior year in high school, James and his guys, representing the Shooting Stars, were entered in the Mac Irvin Summer Basketball Classic in Chicago. James was back in a basketball milieu. NBA scouts were on hand taking notes and several pros, from Eddy Curry to Shawn Marion, dropped by to investigate the doings. The Shooting Stars opened with a 68–64 victory over Team Minnesota and James pleased the crowd of about 1,000 spectators by scoring 17 points and passing for 10 assists. He posed for pictures and also signed autographs on T-shirts, dollar bills, and a woman's pink gym shoes.

The Shooting Stars' second tournament game began about 90 minutes later in a match-up against The Rising Stars (of north suburban Chicago). After a play at the defensive end, James was fed a pass for a fast break. One thing that provoked gasps from fans was the sight of James in the open court, dribbling at full speed with either no defenders or one defender between him and the basket. On this play, planning a thundering dunk, James leapt from the foul line. About 15 feet from the hoop, one player on defense held his ground. James flew high, but the defender stood still. The two collided and James flipped and landed on his back, hitting the hardwood forcefully.

James did not rise quickly. He rolled onto his stomach and his face displayed agony. The gym at Julian High School hushed as teammates ran to his aid. James was led off of the court and soon was taken to a hospital a short distance away by a fire department emergency technician. Later after James was transferred to Northwestern Memorial Hospital, a nurse told reporters that James had suffered a broken left wrist. At the time, 11 minutes and 19 seconds remained in a game that the Ohio club was winning, 53–22. After James was escorted from the premises, play was not resumed, the Chicago team coach said, because some fans were making threatening statements to the player whose accidental defensive stop knocked down James.[14]

James's left arm was in a cast and his summer basketball season was over just as it was starting. Doctors predicted he would be unable to play ball for between six and eight weeks. Although he had already decided not to play football, the basketball injury was a reminder of the type of risk he would have run in that sport. As everyone told him, there was too much at stake in basketball to bother with football anymore except for watching it on TV and listening to John Madden.

If James was off the summer circuit playing for the Shooting Stars, he never sank below the radar in the basketball world. Fans did not see him in games and sports-page readers may not have paid any attention to details of off-the-court games swirling around James, but there were James developments. Although he couldn't play basketball anymore during the summer before his senior year, the injury was not expected to have long-term effects. James was just as hot a commodity for the future as he had been. Although James had followed protocol and taken the ACT test required for college-bound students in Ohio, by then everyone knew that James was less likely to become a Tar Heel than a Celtic.

Instead of playing basketball, James received full-court lobbying treatment from Nike and adidas, both basketball shoe companies seeking the inside track to sign him up for millions of dollars once he was no longer an amateur. James had been scheduled to play at the adidas summer camp, but once he got hurt, he decided to attend both the adidas and Nike summer camps in person—in street clothes. It was one of those wisdom-of-Solomon decisions designed to avoid showing favoritism.

That was a good idea in theory, but for once James miscalculated media and public reaction when he agreed to appear for a press conference at the adidas camp. He arrived an hour late, wearing an adidas headband and Nike wrist bands (so good so far), but also displaying a "King James" T-shirt. The combination of tardiness and the T-shirt did not make a good first impression on media members who did not know James and were predisposed to think of him as arrogant or spoiled. When James and his mom checked into the hotel, the King James T-shirt awaited him. James flippantly commented that it was in his room, and added, "God gave it to me."[15] No one at the press conference would have disputed a James statement that he had God-given talent, but some took offense to this so-called God-given gift.

"The reviews were brutal," early James biographer Ryan Jones wrote.[16] James has always been honest and his answers to certain questions were read differently by those who had never heard him talk before. "The shoe companies flew him back and forth across the country, the media put demands on his time and made money off his fame," Jones wrote, "potential agents whispered promises and introduced him to their star clients—and through it all, LeBron James was supposed to act like the same poor, anonymous kid from Akron, grateful for the attention and content to go quietly back to that same small apartment every night."[17]

If James was bruised by the brief media onslaught, he did not show it much. By the middle of August, the cast came off his wrist. It had healed as quickly as possible. So James immediately returned to the court to test the bone's strength. There was nothing scheduled for the Shooting Stars, but James was invited to a Michael Jordan kids' basketball camp in Santa Barbara as a counselor. James's old St. Vincent teammate Maverick Carter, who had played one season for Western Michigan and then transferred to the University of Akron and had become an even closer friend, was there, too. Gradually, Carter evolved into James's man Friday, a buffer separating him from pushy fans, a helpmate who could watch James's back. Carter later said that James was as popular in some ways as Jordan at the camp. "He signed more autographs than Mike," Carter said.[18]

Sometimes forgotten was the fact that James had come from nothing, that only a few years before he became the basketball world's darling, he and Gloria had shuffled from house to house trying to escape poverty. But James never forgot. Even though he was not raking in cash yet since he was still a high school player, whenever he could he participated in charitable activities. Near the end of his junior year, James arrived at school toting a bag of various types of basketball shoes and sweat clothes. Conducting a trivia contest in the cafeteria at lunchtime, James gave all of the goodies to his schoolmates.

FAMOUS EVERYWHERE

In late summer, just before the beginning of senior year, James and his mother organized another kind of LeBron giveaway. Approximately 600 youngsters at the Akron Community Service Center and the Urban League were presented with James's autograph, a message on the importance of education, LeBron bookmarks, plus backpacks, folders, and notebooks. The shoe companies paid for everything. The bookmarks have taken on a bit of fame in James lore, not because of the item, but because of what he had imprinted on them for the kids. He wrote, "My achievements in basketball have made me famous, but if I didn't do the work in the classroom, you would never know who I am."[19] Many athletes say that children should have role models and heroes besides sports figures. James, who had a 3.0 grade point average on a scale of 4.0, embraced the idea of being a role model from an early age. Even as a 17-year-old he understood that some kids were going to look up to him regardless of what other adults or athletes advised.

After James's truncated summer because of the broken wrist, and without football to occupy him in the fall, James was anxious for basketball to begin. Early in the school year, St. Vincent-St. Mary made basketball news without James's involvement, even though the developments were totally built around him. The school announced that once again home games would be played at the University of Akron's Rhodes Arena. No surprise there. It was reported that the high school took in $268,735 in gate receipts from the Ohio games during James's junior year. In addition, the school received as much as $10,000 in appearance fees for competing in those tournaments around the nation.[20]

Senior year was definitely going to be a frequent-flyer season for James and his friends. The Fighting Irish were scheduled to play in Los Angeles, Pittsburgh, Philadelphia, New Jersey, and North Carolina. There were six teams on the schedule ranked in *USA Today*'s top 25, including No. 1 Mater Dei of California. St. Vincent-St. Mary was ranked No. 10 and James, Joyce, Cotton, McGee, and Travis wanted the chance to prove themselves and move up to the top ranking. They had the chance to see the country and play many of the nation's best high school teams. If newspaper columnists thought this was exploitation of James and his teammates, the players loved the idea of how much fun travel would be. Some clamored about St. Vincent "greed." Some games at Rhodes Arena cost $50 for selected tickets. And 10 St. Vincent Ohio games were to be shown throughout the region on pay cable TV.

St. Vincent school officials defended the moves by saying more local fans wanted to see LeBron James play high school basketball than even the move to the larger Akron arena could accommodate. And the players deserved to test themselves against the best competition available at their level of play. Just try convincing 17-year-old high school basketball players that regularly showcasing their talents on TV was a bad thing!

NOTES

1. David Lee Morgan, Jr., *The Rise of A Star—LeBron James* (Cleveland: Gray & Company Publishers, 2003), p. 90.

2. Morgan, p. 89.

3. Ryan Jones, *King James: Believe the Hype—The LeBron James Story* (New York: St. Martin's Press, 2003), p. 87.

4. B.J. Robinson, *LeBron James—King of the Court* (East Cleveland: Forest Hill Publishing, 2005), p. 50.

5. Robinson, p. 49.

6. Robinson, p. 58.

7. Robinson, p. 56.

8. Robinson, p. 66.

9. Jones, p. 112.

10. Morgan, p. 92.

11. Jones, p. 115.

12. Morgan, p. 96.

13. Barry Temkin, *Chicago Tribune*, June 9, 2002.

14. Temkin, June 9, 2002.

15. Robinson, p. 82.

16. Jones, p. 138.

17. Jones, p. 140.

18. Jones, p. 140.

19. Robinson, pp. 83–84.

20. Morgan, p. 100.

Chapter 4

SENIOR YEAR
BASKETBALL CIRCUS

There are many ways to measure success. Some people add up dollars. Some people figure fame tells all. Some people rate status symbols, like how many big toys a guy can fit into his driveway, from a fancy car to a boat. And then there are smaller measurements that resonate in the telling if not in the bank account. James could claim something that possibly no other high school athlete in history could—there was a LeBron James bobble-head doll for basketball fans. James said having a bobble-head of his likeness made him very proud.[1]

The schedule, the pay TV (at $7.95 per game), the high ticket prices, the bobble-head doll, all heralded a wild and frantic senior year for James. But not even he could have guessed how crazy things would get.

As the start of the 2002–03 Ohio high school basketball season approached, St. Vincent came under attack from an unexpected source. Clair Muscaro, the commissioner of the Ohio High School Athletic Association, the governing body that oversees all high school sports in the state, was annoyed by the Fighting Irish's ambitious schedule. He did not like the idea of Ohio high school players gallivanting around the country playing teams from other states in front of big arena crowds. He suggested maybe the school was overdoing things. Muscaro was a powerful man, not someone to cross if a school wanted to stay eligible for playoffs, or to make sure its players were eligible.

"I felt (LeBron) was exploited through all the travel out of state and across the country," Muscaro said. "It's not what we are about. It should be about hopping in the yellow school bus and going 30 to 45 miles to play in a gym and then coming home again. It should not be about flying and limousines and promoters making money."[2]

Muscaro's stern comments proved inflammatory among those who felt they were in the midst of the time of their lives lapping up heretofore unheard of opportunities for a small private school in Akron. But his comments appealed to high school sports purists who felt things had gotten out of hand with James and other teams in other sports. Sports had lost their proper place in the curriculum, they felt, and some applauded Muscaro. On the other side of the argument were people who felt Muscaro was hopelessly out of date, that what St. Vincent-St. Mary was doing was simply taking advantage of invitations to participate in high-profile events open to high schools who were good enough. This was the modern way of doing things and it wasn't fair to hold back James or St. Vincent. There was an undercurrent of belief that Muscaro was also the front man for coaches, players, and parents affiliated with other Ohio schools that were jealous of the praise and attention lavished on James and St. Vincent, that he was the mouthpiece for the under-the-surface complainers about James's stature. Whispered about, but left unsaid in public, was whether race was an issue. Would suspicions have been raised if James was white?

Muscaro's first volley incited a war of words with St. Vincent Coach Dru Joyce II, who defended the school and his players vociferously. "Clair cannot look me in the eye and tell me to my face that I exploited LeBron James or my players," Joyce said.[3]

Joyce knew how much sweat and work went into molding this team. He was there from the beginning, when the same youngsters won age-group titles. He knew these guys better than anyone else, and it was no stretch or fib for him to point out that although they might be having fun as they toured the country, they were mostly motivated by the chance to become a national high school champion. Besides, from a technical standpoint, unless St. Vincent broke rules, Muscaro and his association shouldn't have a beef with them.

Certainly, any old-fashioned high school fan could not identify with the royal treatment received by James and his teammates as they moved about the country. By the time they reached Los Angeles to play Mater Dei, the Fighting Irish were ranked No. 1 in the nation. They were transported by limousine. The game was scheduled for 14,000-seat Pauley Pavilion, home of storied UCLA. The team dined at Lawry's prime rib restaurant in Beverly Hills. It would not be hard to ask, how much is too much? And it was not out of line for an official like Muscaro to examine reports of such a trip and wonder if such fancy treatment was appropriate for high school boys. But were any high school association rules broken? Not to anyone's knowledge.

Still, there were valid questions. LeBron James was in the right place at the right time, with the right school, and the right talent. It was almost as if high school basketball had been waiting for a messiah to come along and make the final breakthrough to the national mainstream stage. Although it was suggested that James was packaged by his coach and school, such a thing cannot be simply arranged. The player at the vortex of the issue and in the forefront of the promotion must be the real deal or he will quickly be exposed. James was not a natural self-promoter. He was thrust into the role and grew practiced at dealing with the media and in accepting the platitudes and his exciting opportunities. Although cynics abounded, James managed to keep up with his school work and post good grades. As James's reputation as a top-notch player spread, and as the opinion that he was someone who could become the next great NBA player became ingrained in public consciousness, the demand to see him play exploded.

Early in the summer, before he broke his wrist, James had participated in a workout with the Cleveland Cavaliers at the invitation of Coach John Lucas. Although James showed well and established players raved about him, this was against the rules. The NBA had a rule against working out players who were not draft eligible. Lucas compounded his error by telling the *Cleveland Plain Dealer*, "We got to have him."[4] NBA Commissioner David Stern fined Lucas $150,000 and suspended him for the first two games of the league season when it began in November. No one could blame the Cavaliers for wanting a close-up look at James, but cynical Cavs fans figured this was just another screw-up by a team that seemed to lead the league in bad luck and costly mistakes.

Was James wrong for accepting an invitation to test himself against the local pros? It was only a workout and he did nothing wrong in the eyes of high school authorities. It was Lucas who was smacked with the penalty because he was supposed to know NBA rules.

There was a natural progression in the attention on James. First, St. Vincent games sold out the tiny home game at the school. Then St. Vincent games sold out the larger University of Akron arena. Then St. Vincent games sold out major city arenas around the country. There was more demand than supply. More fans than could readily drive to a LeBron James game in person wanted to see LeBron James play right now, not wait until he turned pro. That's how it came to pass that St. Vincent-St. Mary's third game against Oak Hill Academy in late 2002 was televised by ESPN2.

BIG-TIME NATIONAL TV

The game was scheduled for December 12, 2002, at the Cleveland State University Convocation Center. Scouts from 10 NBA teams attended, presumably to watch championship caliber basketball and to take notes about up-and-coming talent on the two teams. If LeBron James had been sunning himself on a beach in Florida, however, none of them would have come. The network's choice of announcers advertised that the event was of major import in the basketball world. Dick Vitale, the prominent voice of college basketball, teamed with Bill Walton, the former college and pro star who analyzed NBA ball. The Fighting Irish had lost twice to the Virginia school in recent years and really felt this time it was their turn to post the victory.

And that's how it played out. James scored 31 points to lead the Irish to the revenge win, 65–45. He seasoned his performance with the occasional spectacular dunk that made fans spill their popcorn, but kept his cool and his statements low key when asked about his starring role. The self-effacing comments struck the right tone. James might showboat with a fancy shot once in a while for fun, but the buying public really did think it was all about James putting on a show. That's why they spent their money. Quite a few did plunk down some bucks to watch, too, including 11,523 in the building and another 1.77 million on television.

Vitale, who has spent a quarter of a century as the colorful commentator on college ball and who long ago coached in the NBA and in college, was pumped for his thoughts as a man who has seen every player of stature for so long. "The curiosity is overwhelming," the enthusiastic Vitale said. "It's a runaway train because of the hype, but he's even better than I expected, and I expected a lot."[5]

In other words, if you asked the most authoritative voice in college basketball if LeBron James could play, he was going to tell you to buy season tickets to your favorite NBA team because James was never going to spend a minute in college. Ironically, although he was only turning 18 two weeks after the Oak Hill game, James looked much older. Pictures of James as a freshman and sophomore, before his body filled out with muscle, before he attained his full height, and before his face lost some of its softness, make him look like an overgrown kid. By his senior year, James had matured in every way, and he resembled a college senior going on 22. This appearance was appropriate, though, as his game was at least four years ahead of his age in quality.

For better or worse, the spotlight never shone brighter on any high school athlete than on LeBron James. "It is hard to remain just a kid, though, when you are acclaimed as the No. 1 high school basketball player in the nation and deemed to be so gifted you might have been the No. 1 pick in last June's draft had you only finished high school and been therefore old enough to enter it," wrote *Chicago Tribune* high school sports columnist Barry Temkin at about the time James geared up for his national television debut. "And so it is that the life of LeBron James, high school basketball player, has become a maelstrom of activity unprecedented in high school sports."[6]

According to Temkin's perusal of eBay, the Internet auction site, at the moment he wrote his story, there were more than 200 LeBron James items up for bid, including an autographed basketball that had passed $300 in bidding. There was a better than even chance that James did not even remember where he signed the ball or for whom.

At about the same time, St. Vincent-St. Mary officials were shaking their heads over the extent to which James had become a phenomenon. Given that no high school athlete had been the subject of so much white-hot focus, it was a mere formality to state that they had never been through this type of attention blitz. "I know he's that good, but I'm still amazed at the amount of attention focused on one high school basketball player," said Dave Rathz, the school headmaster. "We were not ready for this. We have been overwhelmed and surprised every step of the way."[7]

Each time St. Vincent took the court to play basketball under the big top (and the tops were pretty big in major city arenas), it was almost as if the circus had come to town. The atmosphere was expectant—show me a good time—as the audience asked for thrills more than victories. Arenas and gyms were crammed with fans on hand to see the spectacular, not necessarily to see St. Vincent win a well-played game. In many places, outside of their desire to have James show his stuff, the fans might not be rooting for either team.

"James has taken the hype to a new level," Temkin wrote, "perhaps because he is viewed as that player who finally may become 'the next Michael Jordan' and partly because of the unrelenting media spotlight that has trained its sights on him. Whether James is better than the phenoms that came before him is yet to be seen. But he certainly has benefited from being at the right moment in time, with technology and the Internet fueling his mystique."[8]

Sports have become such a national mania that a player like James could be celebrated into mythical status before finishing high school. But the same hype machine and scouting of youngsters extends to other sports, as well. Baseball players are no longer discovered on sandlots, but spend all of their youth competing in summer leagues beyond Little League and attending instructional camps. James made the leap into national consciousness more readily because basketball is not only a wildly popular game at several levels of competition, but because games can so readily be affected by a single player. With only five men on the court at once, the contribution of one superstar is far more likely to make an impact than in other team sports.

LeBron James was neither the brashest nor the shyest of basketball players. He was confident in his abilities because he had proven himself repeatedly. He had been told innumerable times how great he was and how great he would be. Some athletes wilt under pressure and some cringe in the floodlights. By the middle of his senior year, James had clearly grown into his celebrity status. Rather than be cowed by all of the adult activity that might have swallowed him up, James remained calm, but he also made the most of his fame. He took the easy-going approach of "What's not to like?"

If James was in the spotlight, so was his team. The USA Today ratings said St. Vincent-St. Mary was the top-rated team in the land, not LeBron James.

HUMMERGATE

Every high school kid wants wheels. He wants to be able to drive his own car. He wants to be the one in his group who can give the rides. He wants the freedom that sitting behind the steering wheel symbolizes. LeBron James was no different than the typical teenager in that way. Sure he wanted his own car and if he was going by the sobriquet "King James" it should be a suitable chariot.

For most of his life, James and his mother Gloria would not have been able to afford any kind of car. Not even a $400 junker. But given the hype, the attention, and the focus on his basketball talents, it somehow would be a letdown for James to tool around Akron on the city bus. On the other hand, NCAA investigators are trained to look for such flagrant signs of moola changing hands that indicate a young player is being inappropriately enriched. Often the smoking gun shows up as a fancy vehicle seemingly out of the price range of the player's family. Although James would likely never be subject to NCAA scrutiny since he was unlikely to play for an NCAA institution, high falutin' styling cars had become tip-offs to the cynical that something shady was up.

It was understood that within months, after he completed his senior year of basketball, James was going to be a millionaire, signed to a multiyear contract by some lucky NBA team that would pick him in the June draft and that some basketball shoe company would reward James with additional millions.

Still, it raised eyebrows and piqued curiosity when LeBron James's 18th birthday present at the end of December 2002 turned out to be a $50,000 platinum-colored Hummer H2 with chrome rims. It was a show vehicle, for certain. For those who considered James too good to be true, this was an "aha" moment. If James and his mom were so poor, how could they afford a fancy vehicle?

The Hummer was something worthy of being seen in. If people didn't recognize the guy at the wheel before, they definitely did as soon as the gift became the object of media attention. The story, as told by James and his mother, was that she wanted to get him something special and was able to take out a bank loan for the purchase price. It was lost on no one that, probably only two years before, her financial circumstances would have precluded Gloria taking out any type of substantial loan. This could be termed rags to riches, literally. If the simplest story the Jameses told was the whole truth, then Gloria was putting up her son's basketball ability as collateral. And the bank most assuredly saw it as a good risk.

"Hummergate" would not rest there. Once again the Ohio High School Athletic Association showed interest, wondering if James's amateur standing was compromised. Did some professional agent buy it for him? If so, his high school career could be ended abruptly by an ineligibility ruling. "The thing I'm concerned about was that it was a gift from the outside," said Commissioner Clair Muscaro. "When our association sees something like that it throws up a red flag."[9]

St. Vincent-St. Mary officials agreed to investigate and report to the association. Whether or not the gift was an innocent gesture made possible by Gloria's newly appreciated status as LeBron's mom, it was in some ways an inadvisable purchase, certain to provoke inquiries. James, who by this time in his high school career was a seasoned interviewee by the media and believed he had been through every type of inquisition, dreamed up his own casual response to the controversy. At a Rhodes Arena game against an Ohio team as the questions unfolded, James appeared on the floor and raced a toy Hummer around the court using hand-held controls. The real Hummer, he joked, while laughing.

The James Hummer caper was front-page news in the *Cleveland Plain-Dealer*. That put pressure on the Ohio association to look into the matter, whether or not Muscaro was disposed to do so—though he seemed perfectly willing to play the heavy. The better part of a month went by, taking the season to the end of January, before it was announced that no rules violations were found. There was no proof that James was given a valuable present by anyone other than his mother. It was just another chapter in the ongoing soap opera of Life with LeBron.

PLAYING THE BEST IN THE U.S.

Between fending off rumors about his life and going to class, James played some basketball. The Fighting Irish seemed to be as good as *USA*

Today advertised, whipping past opponents with ease, whether they were from Ohio or other parts of the country. The Irish crushed Detroit Redford, 76–41, in Cleveland (30 points for LeBron), and mashed Mentor High, 92–56, in Akron. That was the night James played with his remote controlled Hummer on the gym floor. Then he toyed with the opposition, scoring a high-school career high 50 points. In Greensboro, North Carolina, St. Vincent overpowered RJ Reynolds High School, 85–56. Back in Ohio, the Irish thumped Walsh Jesuit, 98–46, in their final home game in Akron, and bested Buchtel, 82–71.

The more famous an athlete, actor, or other celebrity becomes, the more likely his movements are compared to those of Elvis Presley and the Beatles when they were in their primes. It has become part of the lexicon to say that someone is being accorded "rock star" treatment. In other words, every move made is subject to being overrun by mobs. Those who make big money and are concerned for their safety hire bodyguards. James was still a high school basketball player without an income, but as time passed he needed help to squeeze through crowds.

Darrell Hill was chief of security at the apartment building where the Jameses lived. Sometimes he even traveled on the road with St. Vincent. Tellingly, as an indicator of just how big James had become, media were often camped outside his front door. To help James elude the onslaught, Hill sometimes abetted a subterfuge, placing James body doubles in the Hummer and driving it out to the street. The car left and so would the reporters. Then James was free to go as he pleased.[10]

JERSEYGATE

Soon routine stakeouts of James's home were the least of his worries. At the end of January 2003, James, who was partial to the type of athletic "throwback" jerseys popular among sports fans, joined some friends on a visit to Next Urban Gear and Music, a Cleveland store. Throwback jerseys depict former uniform styles of professional sports teams and sometimes feature the name of a famous retired or deceased player on them. The trend is to make old-fashioned stuff seem fresh. James had been in the store before, and being sports fans themselves, the operators recognized him. They cut a deal with James. In exchange for some autographs, they traded him some jerseys. It sounded fair to James and he consummated the agreement.

The arrangement quickly became public and once again the Ohio High School Athletic Association opened an investigation into James's behavior, declaring that if he had accepted something of value for free, he could be suspended for the rest of the season. James was given a replica jersey of former Chicago Bear Hall of Fame running back Gale Sayers and former NBA star Wes Unseld valued at a combined $845. Within one day the association ruled that James was guilty of violating its rules, and he could never play again for St. Vincent. The association also demanded that St. Vincent forfeit its win over Buchtel because the infraction occurred before that game.

"In talking with the store's personnel, I was able to confirm that on January 25 the merchant gave clothing directly to James at no cost," Muscaro said. "This is a direct violation of the OHSAA bylaws on amateurism because, in fact, LeBron did capitalize on athletic fame by receiving these gifts."[11] There was no report indicating the merchants returned the autographs, and if so, Muscaro's thoughts represented a dramatic misreading of the sports memorabilia market. It's probable in the present-day marketplace that James autographs are now more valuable than the jerseys.

The incident confirmed just how much James was under public scrutiny and how his behavior had better be on par with a choirboy's if he was to avoid criticism. There were always morality police on guard. In this instance, James displayed unsophisticated judgment, and he paid a price.

James returned the jerseys and issued a public apology. Fred Nance, a well-known community lawyer, appealed the case for the Jameses while St. Vincent kept James on the sidelines for its next game against Canton McKinley, another Ohio school. Outside the school, one protester wearing a paper bag over his head held a sign reading, "Free LeBron."

With James in street clothes acting as a cheerleader in the first missed game of his high school career, the Irish outlasted their foe, 63–62. Athletes and sports writers railed against the James season-long suspension. One basketball agent suggested it was like trying Al Capone for income tax invasion. Some writers suggested James was being persecuted by the envious.

Summit County Court took up the case and issued a temporary ruling that allowed James to play again. The Court upheld forfeiture of the Buchtel game and determined justice would best be served by a two-game James suspension, the missed game against Canton McKinley, plus one. It was somewhat of a Solomonesque ruling, not absolving James of wrongdoing, but sentencing him to time served, while overruling the state association's broad punishment decree.

ANOTHER TITLE

Once James was out of the courtroom and back on the court, he shone brighter than ever. His first game following the newly christened

"Jerseygate" affair was actually played in New Jersey. The Irish faced Los Angeles Westchester in the Prime Time Shoot Out in Trenton, New Jersey. A fired-up James, wanting to show that he was back operating on all cylinders, pumped in 52 points, his new career high, as St. Vincent won, 78–52. Before the state tournament Coach Dru Joyce II scheduled an extra game against Akron Firestone to fulfill the last of James's suspension requirements. James did not play, but his high school No. 23 jersey was retired at the game. Before the state tournament the court issued a final ruling allowing James to play and indicating James and St. Vincent had been punished sufficiently by the Ohio association.

Burned in the finals the year before, St. Vincent was on a mission to win its third state title during the four years of the LeBron era. The Irish opened with an 84–30 victory over Kenmore, won their fourth straight district championship, and worked their way to the state final once again. The Irish were focused, hustled on defense, and deferred to James on offense while playing Kettering Alter at a slowdown pace. It was not a game for the highlight films, but St. Vincent prevailed, 40–36. James scored 25 of the winning team's total.

The result of the game mattered far more than the ugliness of play, and the days surrounding the March 22, 2003, championship contest were significant for LeBron James in many ways. He had ascended to such stature in his sport that, as his high school career wound down, the Naismith Basketball Hall of Fame in Springfield, Massachusetts, requested one of his game jerseys. One day it would be a throwback jersey itself. Ohio school athletic officials voted James the boys' high school basketball player of the year for the third time. It was an unprecedented accomplishment. And despite all of the ups and downs with the forfeit, Hummergate, and Jerseygate, USA Today declared St. Vincent-St. Mary the No. 1 high school team in the nation.

LeBron James's high school basketball career—for that matter, his life—already had been a longer journey, with strange interludes of both magnificence and disappointment. It was easy to forget he was still just 18 years old. But no one forgot for a moment that he was on a path that would likely lead to great riches and great sporting achievements. James sounded reflective when reviewing his high school experience.

"I think of my career as a roller coaster," he said. "There's been ups, there's been downs, there's been double loops." When asked what was next, James laughed and said, "What's next is . . . party tonight!"[12]

Four years of high school were in the books. The country could calm down, except for the fans who couldn't wait to see LeBron James on a basketball court playing for a professional team.

NOTES

1. Mark Stewart, *Star Files—LeBron James* (Chicago: Raintree Publishing, 2006), p. 20.

2. David Lee Morgan Jr., *The Rise of A Star—LeBron James* (Cleveland: Gray & Company Publishers, 2003), pp. 99–100.

3. Morgan, p. 100.

4. Ryan Jones, *Believe the Hype—The LeBron James Story* (New York: St. Martin's Press, 2003), p. 130.

5. B. J. Robinson, *LeBron James—King of the Court* (East Cleveland: Forest Hill Publishing, 2005), p. 92.

6. Barry Temkin, *Chicago Tribune*, December 6, 2002.

7. Temkin, December 6, 2002.

8. Temkin, December 6, 2002.

9. Robinson, p. 107.

10. Jones, pp. 168–169.

11. Robinson, p. 111.

12. Robinson, pp. 120–121.

Chapter 5

THE LEBRON SWEEPSTAKES

By the spring of 2003, it was apparent that the worst (or no better than second worst) team in the NBA was the Cleveland Cavaliers, LeBron James's hometown team and, at 40 miles away, the team closest to his home of Akron. The Cavaliers finished their 82-game season with a record of 17 wins and 65 losses. That record equaled the Denver Nuggets for futility.

Descriptions of the Cavaliers' competency ranged from "horrible" to "terrible" to "hopeless." If you wanted to watch bad basketball, you journeyed to Ohio and purchased always-plentiful tickets to Cavs games. It was more painful than putting up with a toothache. It is easier for a team to get well in professional basketball, however, than it is in other professional sports because only five men can play at once. A single important draft pick amounts to 20 percent of the starting lineup. In football, there are 22 starters, counting offense and defense. In baseball, it often takes several years for a first-round draft pick to mature into an on-field talent. Although the situation in the National Hockey League has been changing lately, historically, first-rounders need a couple of years of seasoning to make it.

For decades, the NBA had a clear-cut rule—the team that finished with the league's worst record during the regular season had the overall first pick in the next draft. Over time, however, league officials grew suspicious of the effort being put into the season's final games by bottom feeders with nothing to lose in the standings, but everything to lose by suddenly playing themselves out of the top draft pick. Therefore the league instituted a draft lottery. All of the teams weak enough to

miss out on the playoffs were lumped together. Gradually, the procedure evolved into a system with ping-pong balls. The team with the
worst record had its name written on the largest number of ping-pong
balls, giving it the best odds to gain the best reward. There were 1,000
balls and the team with the worst record was awarded 250, a 25 percent
chance of gaining the top pick. Because Cleveland and Denver tied,
they each were given 225 balls (a 22.5 percent chance of obtaining the
first selection). But some mediocre team that missed the playoffs by a
hair and had its name written on many fewer ping-pong balls could still
win the top prize.

In some years, a franchise-saving player may not be available and it
might not make much of a difference if a team drafted first, second, or
third. The 2003 draft was not one of those years. The presence of James's
old competitive friend Carmelo Anthony, who entered the draft after playing one season for Syracuse, notwithstanding, it was obvious that LeBron
James was the consensus No. 1 pick, the player who could alter a team's
destiny. It was coincidental that nearby Cleveland was the team most de-
serving of the first pick. James had national basketball fame by the end of
his high school career, but he was very much a household name in the
Cleveland-Akron area. Not only did James, who averaged 31.6 points, 9.6
rebounds, and 4.6 assists his senior year, possess the type of talent that
could quickly turn around the team's fortunes on the court (with a little
help from his friends), but he had the charisma and name recognition to
produce major box office rewards instantly.

Although James occasionally floated names of colleges on an ever-
changing list, hardly anyone believed that James intended to play college
basketball. The controversial, seemingly nit-picking officious acts that
dogged him because he drove around in his mother's flashy birthday present and the hassles that followed over Jerseygate virtually sealed the deal.
If that was the situation in high school, what type of battle would it be
to retain eligibility in college with the NCAA breathing down his neck
all of the time? It was also apparent that a basketball shoe company was
prepared to pay James millions of dollars as fast as a wire transfer could be
accomplished after he announced he was turning pro. The money was too
great to bypass.

If anyone needed a hint on the direction James intended to take, no
road map was necessary. Under NCAA rules, James could play in only two
summer all-star games after his senior year if he intended to be eligible
for college play. Before the end of the school year, James announced that
he planned to play in three all-star games that summer. He could always
change his mind. He could always back out of one game. But playing in

all three indicated to those in the know that James was going to be in the NBA, not under the jurisdiction of the NCAA, the next fall.

BABY NEEDS NEW SHOES

Escalation in the shoe wars followed. James was coveted by Nike, Reebok, and adidas, all key players in the basketball shoe marketplace. Those major companies wanted James's name on a long-term contract to endorse their shoes. For years the companies made deals with famous pro players; Michael Jordan's association with Nike was the most prominent and lucrative. They also made deals with college coaches to outfit their teams. The biggest market was tapping the wallets of the average Joe, the average player who wanted to wear the best shoe for his game, or who wanted to make the loudest fashion statement in his neighborhood. Typically, the shoes were manufactured overseas with cheap labor and sold for $100 to $200 to the American consumer. That combination produced huge profit margins. Jordan was retired and the shoe companies sought the next Jordan, the player whose name would be flashed in the brightest lights and whose performance, personality, and charisma linked him to the have-to-have-them trendy teenage shoe buyer. It didn't really matter to a shoe company what team LeBron James played for (although they would have been thrilled if he landed in New York or Los Angeles) because they were sure his name and game transcended location.

The companies wooed LeBron and Gloria in a variety of ways. Adidas actually put up subtle billboards around Akron (if such an action can be termed subtle) containing low-key messages urging James to choose that company. Consumer advocate Ralph Nader, angered by the shoe companies' dependence on overseas low-paid workers, lobbied James to join him in a global fight for justice.[1] That would have been a biting-the-hand-that-feeds-him approach for James, as he was not even under contract to a shoe company at the time.

In his spare time, in-between visiting shoe company headquarters and taking meetings with shoe company executives, James played in three (count 'em, three) high school all-star games. He competed in the McDonald's All-American game in Cleveland, the Roundball Classic in Chicago, and the Jordan Brand Capital Classic in Washington, D.C. James had not announced his plans to declare himself eligible for the NBA draft as the May 12 deadline loomed, but by participating in all three contests, he had all but officially announced his intentions in another manner. James's high school career was over. He would never have a college career. The 18-year-old Ohio star was going pro.

James was constantly asked about his professional preferences, as if he could close his eyes, point his index finger at a map and choose a city to play in. He was careful to respect all the contenders and joked that it would be nice if the NBA put a franchise in the Bahamas.

Other big-name athletes have not been above orchestrating trades to cities where they preferred to play from cities where they had no desire to put down roots. Denver Broncos football Hall of Fame quarterback John Elway refused to report to the Baltimore Colts. Current quarterback Eli Manning told the San Diego Chargers not to draft him because he didn't want to play in the California city. He was traded to the New York Giants. When Chinese center Yao Ming entered the draft, his country's officials threatened to hold him back if he was not drafted by a team in a city that seemed right for him.

In time for the NBA May 12 deadline and in time for the May 22 lottery distribution of picks, James made his commitment to go pro. He held a press conference at St. Vincent-St. Mary, standing in front of a podium and in front of a backdrop cloth with the words "LeBronJames.com" plastered all over it. There was now a James Web site with all the news that was fit to print about the hoops star available 24 hours a day.

He was not alone, either. James signed with agent Aaron Goodwin to represent him not only with his first NBA contract, but in sifting through and choosing the proper endorsements offering the best deal, shoe contract and beyond. Goodwin was a lower key agent with a less flamboyant reputation than some other agents for NBA players, but he had enough of a stable of good players to make an impression on James and his mother. Among Goodwin's other hoops clients were Gary Payton, a likely future Hall of Famer, and Jamal Crawford. Goodwin said he quietly spent a year lobbying James and his mother, all of the wooing going on out of the spotlight.

LeBron James had spent four years tantalizing basketball coaches, fans, and scouts, showing off his precocious play for St. Vincent and eventually making news wherever he traveled. But with Goodwin in his corner, James was about to drop a bombshell. Peace ended the shoe wars, a winner had been declared. James was going Nike, the powerful Oregon-based company that already owned about 39 percent of the sports shoe market according to an industry source, *Sporting Goods Intelligence*.

That Nike had beaten out adidas and Reebok was not earth shattering. But the price was boggling. The player who had never spent a minute on a college court and didn't even know which professional team he would be affiliated with signed a seven-year, $90-million deal with Nike that included a $10 million signing bonus. The poor little boy who had been shunted from home to home with his mom as a youth was now a rich man. For nearly a year there had been newspaper speculation that LeBron James's signature on a shoe contract might be worth $20 million or so. Riches beyond most people's comprehension, for certain, but that proved to be a gross underestimate, practically pocket change in comparison to the reality. James might be able to afford to buy the Hummer factory before he ever played a minute of NBA ball.

James was joined in sponsorship partnership not only with Nike, but with his long-time basketball hero Jordan, and Tiger Woods, the best golfer on the planet. That wasn't all. As an aside, James signed a contract with Upper Deck, one of the sports card manufacturers that made basketball cards, for $1 million.

James had not yet graduated from high school, and on the day the Nike agreement was announced he did not skip school. He drove to classes in his Hummer and for one more day tried to be a normal high school student. Later that day, the NBA conducted its draft lottery. There were 13 teams in the lottery, the bottom segment of the league. Lottery day is peculiar. It is televised, as are so many off-the-field professional sports moments these days. Unlike the draft, when general managers and team presidents confer on hotlines and handle the serious business of improving their franchises, team officials take a lighter approach to lottery proceedings. Because the outcome depends on chance, there is nothing they can do to affect it. In recent years it has become trendy to send someone to represent the franchise that is lower on the masthead than general manager or president. Sometimes it is a player. Sometimes it is a former player. Sometimes it is a broadcaster. It is a treat, a reward of sorts, to let that person be the face of the franchise nationally, if only for a day.

STAYING HOME FOR THE NBA

Similarly, NBA Commissioner David Stern did not do the heavy lifting when it came time to assign the teams their draft spots. Then-deputy Commissioner Russ Granik opened envelope after envelope in reverse order, with the 13th selector first.

The winner of the right to pick first was . . . the Cleveland Cavaliers. Some basketball observers had been saying that Carmelo Anthony might be the first pick in the draft over James, but the Cavaliers didn't care if President Grover Cleveland was available, they were committed to James all the way. A team that had fallen on tough times saw the light at the end of the tunnel and that tunnel was lit by a miner's headlamp mounted on the headband of LeBron James.

THE CAVALIERS' GOOD, BAD, AND UGLY

The Cleveland Cavaliers were born out of optimism as an NBA expansion team in 1970 and had reached a level of desperation harkening back to their inept rookie year by 2003. When the Cavs entered the league for the 1970–71 season the majority of their players were castoffs from established teams, players who were made available for free by the older teams. The NBA followed the same basic guidelines other professional leagues follow when welcoming a new team into the brotherhood—the league gouged the Cavs for exorbitant entry fees and permitted the club to choose 10th, 11th, and 12th men who had been sitting on benches for the Seattles, Portlands, and New Yorks.

Major league baseball, the National Football League, and the National Hockey League operate in much the same manner. The theory is that new owners are so thrilled to be accepted into the exclusive league club that they will accept pretty much any onerous conditions placed on them that ensures their new team will not become a winner any time soon. Simultaneously, the new owners are taught that they cannot expect any favors from their fellow owners. This general type of procedure has been followed over and over again in all four leagues for decades. The established owners and leagues hold all of the cards and have the right to grant approval or the power to deny admission to owners of new teams. So the new owners always take what is dished out, grateful to be allowed into the league, but knowing it will be a long haul to build a winning team. As a backdrop to the owner muscle flexing, it is generally understood that the fans in a new city will be so happy to have a team to call their own that they will turn out and fill the arena anyway, even though the team is a loser.

THE BAD NEWS CAVS

The Cavaliers made their debut in the NBA during the 1970–71 season under coach Bill Fitch, who soon enough upon escaping from Ohio won a world title as coach of the Boston Celtics. The Cavs finished with 15 wins and 67 losses, a winning percentage of just more than 18 percent. The truest indicator of just how bad the Cavs were compared to the rest of the league was the team's road record. Playing on opposing courts, Cleveland was 2–37. That really meant that whenever the Cavs traveled there was a much better chance that room service would be delivered in a timely manner than they would win a game. No one was surprised.

More than 30 years later, when the Cavaliers again descended to become just about the worst team in the league, they finished with 17 wins and 65 losses, a winning percentage of just more than 20 percent. Cynical observers suggested that nothing had ever changed, but that was too simplistic a viewpoint. A lot had happened in the Cavaliers' world, even if the team came full circle with disastrous on-court results.

Fitch, a hard-nosed, frequently sarcastic, but funny leader, was determined to make something out of the shaky Cavs' roster. He was a sports lifer, considered to be knowledgeable by NBA administrators, but grumpy by some of his players. Fitch guided the Cavaliers through their first nine seasons in the league, a long tenure for a coach starting out with an expansion franchise. Cavs ownership showed patience as Fitch built. A high point came during the 1975–76 season, when Cleveland finished first in its division with a 49–33 record, made the playoffs, and won a series—each for the first time.

Between the departure of Bill Fitch and the ascension of LeBron James, the Cavaliers employed a creditable cast of winning coaches. Among them was the old point guard genius Lenny Wilkens, who eventually became the winningest coach in league history and one of only three men enshrined in the Basketball Hall of Fame as a player and a coach. Besides Wilkens, whose 1991–92 team finished a club best 57–25 (for the second time), Mike Fratello turned in noteworthy work from the bench, although the future TV commentator sometimes made as big a splash with his wardrobe, his suits repeatedly making him a candidate for the tongue-in-cheek league best dressed award. George Karl claimed a seat on the bench for a couple of years, but he had not yet made his breakthrough as an esteemed coach.

Of the 17 men who have held the title of Cleveland Cavaliers head coach from Bill Fitch to current occupant Mike Brown, only Wilkens and Fratello departed with winning records. Except for a few highlight seasons and games, the Cavaliers became synonymous with losing. When the Cavaliers were at their best in the 1990s, they couldn't get past the Michael Jordan-led Chicago Bulls in their own division.

Until downtown renovation and refurbishment took hold, complete with the addition of a new baseball park, football stadium, and major indoor arena for winter sports, Cleveland itself wallowed in an era of self-doubt. The city was the butt of jokes, ranging from statements that there was nothing to do there, to the long past civic embarrassment (impossible to forget or live down) tied to the time when the Cuyahoga River caught on fire in Cleveland because it was so polluted. Bordering Lake Erie, the city was also insulted by such pithy phrases as "The Mistake on the Lake." And none of that even took into account the horrible psychic blow delivered by the football Cleveland Browns, the real soul of the city, and the local pro team with the grandest heritage, when it packed up its helmets, shoulder pads, and yard markers and fled to Baltimore to become the Ravens. The populace was infuriated and team owner Arthur Modell was hung in effigy.

From a highly regarded sports community, Cleveland had devolved into the city cited by national broadcasters as the town that had gone the longest in crowning a champion in any major sport. When was that? the question went. The answer was, long, long ago, in what seemed to be a galaxy far, far away. There was no NHL hockey in Cleveland, so that was out. The Cavaliers had never won a title, so that was out. The Browns, who were replaced by an expansion team also called the Browns, last won the NFL championship in 1964. And the Indians, the oldest team in the mix, last captured the World Series in 1948. Except for the Chicago Cubs, the Indians were the Major League team that had waited the longest for a title.

Around the league, fans either felt sorry for the Cavaliers because they never accomplished much as a team or didn't think much about them at all, simply relegating them to the bottom of the heap each year as a team that would not make the playoffs. The Cavaliers would have put a sexier model on the floor if they had a superstar whose achievements transcended wins and losses, but despite having high draft picks frequently because of the poor or mediocre record, the Cavaliers seemed unable to select a player who made fans' pulse rates race on a consistent basis.

During Cleveland's inaugural season, 7-foot center Walt Wesley, a nice player, as the phrase is often used, but no star, poured in 50 points in a February game against the old Cincinnati Royals. That stood as the Cavs' single game scoring record for 34 years, until LeBron James cracked it.

Wesley had been acquired from the Bulls in the expansion draft. Among other players who had excelled in college or who had made notable contributions to their NBA teams, but were now expendable because their skills were eroding with age, were Len Chappell, Don Ohl, and Johnny Egan. Guard Butch Beard was a solid player with Atlanta and Bobby Smith, who was nicknamed "Bingo" and came over from the old San Diego Rockets, was a valuable pickup. Smith was the gem of the expansion draft. He played 10 seasons with Cleveland and eventually had his No. 7 jersey retired by the team. The first player ever drafted by the franchise was forward John Johnson, who came out of Iowa.

The theory about how fans would come out to watch poor performance just for the thrill of being able to identify with a professional team never took hold in Cleveland. The novelty of professional basketball in a town featuring the best players in the world (at least on other teams passing through) was something that wore off quickly—like after opening day. Or perhaps before the opener. The Cavs' home gym was the ancient Cleveland Arena, a Depression-era facility that seated 11,000 for basketball. The Cavaliers opened for business on October 28, 1970, in a game against San Diego. The Cavs lost 110–99. If ever a game should be a sellout, the first home game in the history of a franchise would be it. The Cavaliers did not even come close. The game attracted 6,144 fans. It didn't help any that Cleveland immediately established just where it fit in the NBA firmament by losing its first 11 games and 14 of its first 15. Not once during the first season did Cleveland sell out at home. The largest crowd was 8,429, and the average for 41 games was 3,518 fans. In today's NBA, such attendance numbers would provoke emergency meetings of the board of governors despairing over what was to become of the team. There would be suggestions that the Cavaliers be moved to Oklahoma City or Mexico City.[2]

SOME CHEERY CAVS TIMES

Things did improve after the first season and although the Cavs spent four dismal seasons playing in the Cleveland Arena, attendance jumped, with the occasional sellout. Team owners realized almost instantly that the dusty old arena was no place to sell a spanking new product, but it took until the 1974–75 season for Cleveland to move into a new building. The Richfield Coliseum, located in the Cleveland suburbs, never received rave reviews from architectural critics and there were complaints about it being located in the middle of nowhere, about 20 miles from downtown, but the place was serviceable. At capacity, the Richfield site could hold 20,000 people and once in a great while that many showed up.

Over time, the team beefed up with some popular and accomplished players. The first big-name rookie addition joining the Cavs in their second season was Austin Carr, the fabulous scorer from Notre Dame who was famous as an All-American and as a player who helped end one of UCLA's tremendous college winning streaks. Carr, a 6-foot-4 guard, averaged 21.2 points per game as a rookie and became a status player. Not only was he talented, but other teams feared his game and local fans believed in him. Although Carr played very well for Cleveland for a few years, a knee injury slowed him down and eventually curtailed his career.

The injury occurred in 1974 and that served as foreshadowing. It seemed whenever something good happened for the Cavaliers, something bad happened to the Cavaliers as a counterbalance. Much like Carr, North Carolina center Brad Daugherty shone, then petered out prematurely because of injury. The 7-footer was a five-time all-star for Cleveland and was the cornerstone of the lineup in the early 1990s, but was forced to retire because of chronic back problems.

Mark Price, the former Georgia Tech playmaker, was one of the best free-throw shooters in NBA history and the four-time All-Star graced the Cavaliers' roster for nine years, although he also suffered a debilitating knee injury. Power forward Larry Nance was an all-star and forward Craig Ehlo was a super substitute. But sometimes it seemed that years passed without any Cavalier highlight to cheer about. Exciting moments were tarnished by painful memories, particularly the injuries to popular players, but also in selected games.

The all-time Cavalier "ouch" moment in a big game was delivered with hammer-like ruthlessness by Michael Jordan. It was 1989, during the play-offs capping the Cavaliers' then-best-ever 57–25 regular-season. Meeting in the first round of the Eastern Conference playoffs, the Cavs and Bulls were tied with two victories apiece. The winner of the next game—a Cavs home game in Richfield—on May 7, would capture the best-of-five series. In a tight game, with the clock running down, Cleveland, which had an eight-point lead earlier in the fourth quarter, took the lead with three seconds to go. Jordan, who scored 44 points, got the ball just where he wanted to and put up a 15-foot jumper at the foul line that fell through the net at the buzzer, giving Chicago a 101–100 victory.

Jordan had predicted the Bulls would win the series in four games, and he had missed a chance to clinch it the game before. When Craig Ehlo made a lay-up the Cavs believed they had salted away the series and made Jordan eat his words. Instead, a game late, Jordan came through, burnished his legend and tarnished the Cavs' self-esteem.

"I just can't believe he made that shot," Cleveland's Brad Daugherty said. "We did everything right. I just can't believe it. I don't see how he stayed in the air so long. It's the most outstanding shot I've ever seen."[3]

Jordan's timely game-winner was henceforth labeled "The Shot" and is regarded as a great moment in Jordan and Bulls dynasty lore as the Chicago team compiled its six NBA championships. The fact that Daugherty raved about Jordan's air time also meshed with the gushing descriptions of Jordan's style as "Air Jordan."

For the Cavaliers the play went down as a heartbreaker, a what-if moment that was a bull's-eye shot through the chest and wounded the entire franchise. It was a shot that seemed to symbolize the jumpstarting of one team for a glorious, years-long ride, and the demoralization of another team for a years-long decline.

If ever a team hungered for a savior to relieve years of disappointment and frustration, it was the Cleveland Cavaliers as the 2003 NBA draft approached. They did not want LeBron James to change zip codes to Beverly Hills 90210 or anyplace else swanky. They wanted him to stay right at home in Ohio.

THE CAVS GO FOR IT

In the NBA there is such a thing as being a bad team at a good time. If you win the lottery and gain the No. 1 overall draft pick, it is possible that all of the pain and suffering of a terrible year might pay off. If the future was built on a single day, then maybe the past would be quickly forgotten.

There is no overstating how badly the Cleveland Cavaliers' management team wanted the rights to LeBron James. It was enough that he was seen as a budding superstar, a difference maker who could create instant box office. But the fact that he was local, as well, was too good to be true. Cavaliers' officials prayed, schemed, imagined, and willed it to be true that they would obtain the No. 1 pick. They dreamed that they would be outfitting LeBron James in Cavalier red and gold for the 2003–04 season.

The stress of waiting to learn if they would receive the top pick in the draft almost overpowered some Cavaliers' administrators. They knew what the addition of James meant to the team. Carmelo Anthony was wonderful and if they picked Anthony they couldn't go wrong, but James's name made them swoon in anticipation.

By the end of the Cavaliers' disastrous 17–65 2002–03 season, Ohio basketball fans were openly rooting for the team to lose games to ensure the worst record and enhance their chances to get the top pick. Leading up to the last game of the regular season, *Cleveland Plain Dealer* sports columnist Bill Livingston wrote that it was a "must-lose" game.[4] The Cavaliers defeated the Toronto Raptors, which at least proved to Commissioner David Stern that they weren't tanking games to finish higher in the James sweepstakes. That victory created the tie with the Denver Nuggets for the worst record and lowered the percentage of likelihood for Cleveland picking first.

For some reason—fan cynicism being the best explanation—conspiracy theories have surrounded the NBA draft. Some fans, who no doubt root for teams that are not often big winners, express the opinion that the NBA wants all of the biggest stars to play in the biggest markets. They say the draft lottery is rigged in favor of New York, Los Angeles, and Chicago. This body of thought may have its origins in the 1985 draft when All-American center Patrick Ewing was coming out of Georgetown and every team wanted his services. The New York Knicks won the rights to Ewing, and some said the draft was rigged so the league could have a strong team in the Big Apple. But despite the Ewing instance, there is overwhelming evidence that the NBA does not influence outcomes and the conjecture is simply based on fan paranoia. In the 2007 draft, much like 2003, the top two picks, like James and Anthony, were regarded as franchise makers. Greg Oden, the Ohio State center, went to the Portland Trailblazers. Kevin Durant, the Texas forward, went to the Seattle Supersonics. Neither franchise is considered a glamorous one and neither city is considered a major market in the league's hierarchy.

The actual lottery event took place on May 22, 2003, in Secaucus, New Jersey. Cleveland team owner Gordon Gund attended, accompanied by Tad Carper, Cavs vice president of communications. Rarely have so many fans and team officials put up with sweaty palms for so long. As the lottery show dragged on and one team after another learned its numbered fate, the fact that Cleveland's name was not called was good news, but nerve-wracking news nonetheless. It was like being named Miss America. Five left, four left, three left, two left, first runner-up. And when there is only one name left, everyone knows who wins.

FINALLY, GOOD LUCK

The Cleveland Cavaliers won the first pick in the 2003 draft. They won the best possible scenario for a vibrant future. The moment the Cavaliers won by losing, Carper burst from his seat and revealed the contents of a mysterious briefcase he had toted around—it contained a LeBron James No. 23 Cavaliers jersey. So much for the idea that the Cavaliers might consider choosing Carmelo Anthony. The Cavs knew who they wanted and now that they acquired the rights to pick James, they held tight with both hands. The jersey display was a broad act of showmanship (something sorely missing in recent Cavaliers' seasons), but it struck the right tone and it laid Cleveland's cards on the table. Not only did the jersey explain exactly what the Cavaliers planned to do with the No. 1 pick, its presence sent a message to other team owners not to even bother to call the Cavs' office to ask about trading for the pick.

Gordon Gund, the charismatic, blind owner of the Cavaliers, was on the scene because he recognized how big a victory this was for his team and its future. He later reflected on the power of luck and lotteries and what adding LeBron James to the team meant. "I was tremendously excited because I had a very good feeling for what this could mean to the marketplace, for the team, and for our employees," Gund said. "We really needed a pickup, and we couldn't have asked for a better one. There are lots of lotteries—and some of them with very big pots—but I don't think any is bigger than that one."[5]

Instantly, the phones began ringing at Cavaliers' headquarters. A month after the season ended dismally, with an awful record, and no play-off games scheduled, fans were dialing in to buy season tickets. In the month-plus between the moment the Cavaliers won the draft lottery and the time they announced the first pick, they sold thousands of season tickets. Home games would no longer be a lonely experience in Cleveland.

Gund spoke as someone who was invested in the team and had a lot to gain from the acquisition of James. Most of James's friends, relatives, coaches, and teammates were happy that he looked like a sure bet for the Cavaliers. That meant he would be staying in the same back yard and they would be able to watch him play.

It was as if the Cavaliers had won the Powerball lottery. In a way they had, but since Gund already possessed mega-millions, he won something that money couldn't buy. LeBron James was going to make the jump directly from high school basketball to the best league in the world. Even for a guy as smooth and talented as James, that figured to be a problem. Over the years many players had attempted to make the leap. Most of them were centers, very tall, some with prematurely powerful bodies.

Moses Malone was the first player to successfully shift from high school to pro play in 1974. Malone was 6-foot-10 and muscular. He had played high school basketball in Virginia and committed to the University of Maryland. At the last minute he went pro and achieved success. A much lesser known name who took the same chance more than 30 years ago was Bill Willoughby. He would have been better served matriculating at a college. Darryl Dawkins also came out of high school in the 1970s and enjoyed some solid seasons. He emerged as a super personality, if not a superstar, during his days with the Philadelphia 76ers.

More recently, the list of high school players who declared for the pro draft rather than spend a year or more in college included the Los Angeles Lakers' Kobe Bryant and the Boston Celtics' Kevin Garnett. Bryant, a guard from Pennsylvania, was a backup as a rookie and averaged 7.6 points a game. He was only 18 and his youth showed on the court. Bryant matured into perhaps the best player in the league, but it took a couple of seasons. The lanky, 6-foot-10 Garnett averaged more than 10 points as a rookie for Minnesota and quickly adapted his style to become a perennial All-Star. What the numbers indicated, however, was that there was a blending-in period, an adjustment time for high school players to learn the faster-paced NBA game and adapt to playing against bigger, stronger opponents. No one doubted that James would be able to make the necessary adjustment, but no one could predict how long it would take.

Some looked as young as they were when they took the court against veterans who had been in the league for years and who knew the ropes. Some, like Willoughby, were willowy. One thing James had in his favor was his body. He weighed 240 pounds. He was only 18, but he already had a man's body that would enable him to withstand many of the rigors of being pushed around in the foul lane where the rebounding action was at its most furious, and by defensive players. But if basketball in high school had been fun and games (and James tried to portray it that way), basketball where big money is involved is very much a business. There is no rule against having fun, but players at the highest level of the sport are paid millions of dollars to take their competitions seriously. Bill Walton, the former UCLA All-American and pro star turned TV commentator, added a dose of realism to the Cleveland giddiness. "Expectations of LeBron will be huge," Walton said. "It's no longer about milk and cookies. This is about men playing for the ultimate prize in a big man's game."[6]

The Cavaliers had just lived through a depressing season. The franchise was aching for change and James represented an opportunity to put a new face on things and to boost optimism. But one other notable event was taking place at the same time the Cavaliers learned they would be able to draft James. The Cavs fired Coach John Lucas (with a record like his it was probably inevitable) and had a vacancy. James had been friendly with Lucas and appreciated the chance Lucas gave him to work out with Cavalier players, even if it cost the coach big bucks.

THE CAVS MAKE A BIG INVESTMENT

The Cavaliers worked quickly to find a suitable replacement, a coach who could help James grow, a coach with experience and a winning background. This was an important hire. The man who got the job would be the person most directly supervising James during his day-to-day formative stages as a rookie. To a large extent, this person would determine James's playing time, and would make choices about when to leave him in to combat foul trouble and when it was more fruitful to learn by watching from the bench. The Cavaliers wanted to be careful and bring in the right wise man.

When they announced who the new coach would be, heads nodded. Paul Silas was well respected around the league, both from his years as a player with the Boston Celtics and then as a head coach with the Charlotte Hornets. When he was active, Silas was regarded as a hard-nosed player who was an excellent rebounder for his size—6-foot-7. He was seen as a team player willing to sacrifice his own scoring statistics to do the dirty work in the paint, rebounding, playing defense, and going head-to-head with other tough guys. He was a member of Celtics world championship teams and then coached young teams. Silas promised to be a good fit, but this was no ordinary rebuilding job, a tough enough task in any circumstances with a losing team. Silas was also being trusted with the family jewels. He had to both guard them and increase their value. He would be judged not just on his won-loss record, but by how he handled LeBron James's seemingly unlimited potential.

When the actual moment arrived for the NBA draft on June 26, 2003, it seemed as if it had been years in the making, even though it had only been a month since it became known that James was going to be chosen by the Cavaliers. In some ways, it was a long-term production, for James had been playing basketball since he was a toddler and he had been on the national scene for more than three years.

On draft day, James pulled on a white suit over a white shirt, complemented by a white tie. It was a bright outfit and his entire body gleamed as brightly as his smile. James was literally the white knight riding to the rescue of the Cavaliers. The NBA draft was conducted at Madison Square Garden in New York and, as usual, was televised by ESPN. In Cleveland, the Cavaliers hosted a special draft party in the then-named Gund Arena, inviting fans to watch in the confines of the home court. Attendance was 10,017, more than had attended Cavaliers games in person during the early days of the franchise. Every one of those fans knew who the Cavs were going to select, so there was no suspense. But when the choice became reality, and Commissioner Stern announced that indeed James was the property of the Cavaliers, supporters in Cleveland seemed to be reliving New Year's Eve in Times Square. Streamers and confetti were dropped from the ceiling, fans roared, and a band started playing music.

When Cleveland made it official, selecting James with the first pick in the 2003 draft, the player shook hands with Stern and slapped a Cavaliers' baseball cap on his head. He smiled one of his 1,000-watt smiles and posed for still and television cameras. Unlike most players joining the pro ranks, James had already become an instant millionaire through his splashy shoe contract and his deal with Upper Deck sports cards. Officially joining the Cavaliers expanded James's bank account even more. Under the NBA players' union collective bargaining agreement contract with owners, James was locked into a four-year deal with a total value of $12.96 million. He would be paid $4.02 million as a rookie, $4.32 million as a second-year man, and $4.62 million in his third year. The fourth year was an option year. If the team was only mildly satisfied with James's performance, he would get another $4.62 million. If, as expected, James became a superstar, negotiations would begin for a much longer and richer contract.

On the night LeBron James was drafted, he was a happy young man. His career in high school had outstripped his imagination. He had supreme confidence that he could do the job on the basketball court that others felt was worth millions of dollars in salary. He was a homegrown player who knew quite well what was expected of him—and he promised he would come through.

On draft night, James pledged to light up Cleveland "like Las Vegas"[7] with his basketball prowess. It sounded brash, but few doubted he would deliver.

"I think I'll be able to do enough on the court to lift the city of Cleveland," James said in his postdraft news conference.[8] It was a daunting assignment for one so young, but he was a Hercules of the basketball court and since LeBron James had made the aging rust-belt city of Akron feel good about itself, why couldn't he do the same for Cleveland, just up the turnpike?

Austin Carr, the one-time Cavs top scorer whose own injury contributed to the team's hard-luck outlook in the 1970s, cried when Cleveland won the first pick and reflected on the meaning of LeBron the moment Cleveland won the lottery. He felt it was a sign from the basketball gods, he said, that it was at last "Cleveland's turn. You couldn't ask for a better shot in the arm. What happened was like a miracle. The first thing I thought was, 'We finally beat the other cities, we finally are starting to head in the right direction.'"[9]

NOTES

1. David Lee Morgan Jr., *The Rise of A Star—LeBron James* (Cleveland: Gray & Company Publishers, 2003), p. 156.

2. Cleveland Cavaliers 2006–7 Media Guide.

3. Sam Smith, *Chicago Tribune*, May 8, 1989.

4. Roger Gordon, *The Rookie Season of LeBron James* (Champaign, IL: Sports Publishing, 2004), p. 3.

5. Gordon, p. 7.

6. B.J. Robinson, *LeBron James—King of the Court* (East Cleveland: Forrest Hill Publishing, 2005), p. 133.

7. Gordon, p. viii.

8. Gordon, p. vi.

9. Gordon, p. v.

Chapter 6

A ROOKIE, NOT A BEGINNER

Two things were instantly established when LeBron James made his professional debut with the Cleveland Cavaliers on October 29, 2003, in an NBA game against the Sacramento Kings in California. James was not your average rookie. He scored 25 points, passed off for 9 assists, and gathered 6 rebounds in the season opener. And the Cavaliers were not going to be contenders overnight. They lost, 106–92.

Neither the Kings nor the Cavaliers were among the league's elite at the time, and the game drew much more attention than it ordinarily would have by marking a milestone in James's career. There was no mistaking that the spotlight was on James. For years, James dreamed of becoming a professional basketball player. For what seemed like a century, basketball observers had speculated about his future in the pros. Now it was here. Now it was the time to show people what he had. Although James always said he was not fazed by external pressure, there was some pressure on him for his first game. The pressure wasn't so much to lead Cleveland to victory in what was just another regular-season game. Nor was the pressure about his numbers in the box score per se. The pressure was about James fitting in, looking like he belonged, looking like a player who was no longer a high school player, but a prime-time player. James was one of the best players on the court, if not the best, from the get-go. Question No. 1 was answered. Yes, he was ready for the NBA.

"He just mesmerized everybody," said new Cleveland Coach Paul Silas. "He handled everything so well. I just said, 'Wow, if this is the way this is going to be, this kid is just going to set the world on fire.' I had never expected, or really seen, anything like that."[1]

Silas was just another in a long line of coaches, fans, scouts, and basket-ball junkies seduced by the big-time talents of LeBron James at a big-time moment. Of course, Silas hadn't just seen James perform for the first time. In the months after his selection as a Cavaliers draft pick, James spent innumerable hours working on his game, trying to improve, and doing everything he could think of to ready himself for the NBA. It was not as if he lay around on a beach sipping Kool-Aid.

In recent years, NBA clubs have sponsored summer teams for a short season of competition. The rosters generally consist of freshly drafted rookies and free agents who hope to wrangle an invitation to fall training camp and obtain a shot at making the team. In 2003, the Cavs placed James on their summer league team. James had been a fixture on the high school amateur circuit for several summers, but this was different. No lon-ger were his teammates the boys from Akron he grew up with. These teammates were college All-Americans, high pro draft picks, and former college stars trying to break into the NBA after seasoning in Europe or in one of several American minor leagues. Most were hungry players, trying to make a good impression on management. James did not have to worry about that. There was no more of a sure thing that could be bet on in Las Vegas than James making the team. The only thing Cavaliers administra-tors were interested in was James's showing as a progress report.

The NBA track record on the drafting of high school players was sketchy. Few were an immediate sensation. Some were outright busts. Some clearly needed several years of seasoning and were regarded as play-ers who made the wrong choice to enter the draft and who would have been better off going to college. A few years before James was chosen No. 1, the Washington Wizards had selected another player right out of high school, center Kwame Brown, who averaged only in single digits for points scored. Brown did not do well as a rookie and has never blossomed into an NBA star. Cleveland was not comparing James to Brown, but it did want an early peak at its multimillion-dollar investment in game situations.

James turned in solid games in the summer league, scoring 14 points here, 17 points there, and 25 points there. The numbers weren't eye-popping, but he also collected better than average numbers of rebounds and assists. In an intriguing experiment, the Cavaliers tried James at point guard. James was normally a forward, and the maneuver was aimed at learning how he would react if he had the ball in his hands almost all of the time and had the responsibility of involving teammates in the of-fense. James had always excelled at that role. He was regarded as a brilliant passing forward who generally recorded as many assists as a guard, so it was easy to understand why the Cavaliers would try this approach. During the 11-game summer league campaign, James averaged 15.7 points and 4.3 assists a game. The point guard role was not completely abandoned, since the Cavaliers subsequently used James in the job periodically during the ensuing regular season, but it was not a slam-dunk success, either.

James made his greatest impression by the maturity he showed in making judgments on the court, knowing where to throw the ball, when to shoot, and when to pass. He dazzled with his ball handling and slick moves and always lit up the crowd. Officials from other NBA teams, who might not have seen James quite so often as a high schooler or scouted him so heavily since they knew they were not going to receive a high draft pick, marveled at the way he handled himself as an 18-year-old and how he connected with the crowds.

Pat Williams, general manager of the Orlando Magic, raved about James. "He has three attributes that are hard to find in anybody, much less a teenager—maturity, talent, and charisma."[2]

Once the short summer league season wrapped up, there was a lull in James's hectic schedule. He actually had time to rest up before Cavs training camp began on September 26, and he took a vacation in Hawaii between filming some commercials for his new sponsors. Occasionally, however, he emerged from hibernation. James did promote education (as well as dispensing Nike shoes) to fourth and fifth graders in Akron. James and his agent Aaron Goodwin dropped another bombshell when they announced the signing of a six-year endorsement contract with Coca-Cola. The deal called for a $2 million-a-year payment to James. Coca-Cola was a blue chip company and, by declaring its love for James, it made a loud statement in the business world. Companies like Coca-Cola do not take on just any athlete. The contract was a signature statement of belief in James as a national pitchman who could transcend basketball and sports fans with his style, smile, and personality.

An additional sign of how happy the Cavaliers were to select James surfaced when the NBA's television schedule was released for the 2003–04 season. As a team that shared one of the two worst records in the league the season before, the Cavaliers would ordinarily be looked on as one of the league's bottom feeders, a team with little national viewer appeal. The signing of James transformed the Cavaliers' status. Nobody expected Cleveland to challenge for a title in James's first season, but it was expected that he would be the most talked about player in the league and that fan curiosity would demand putting some of his games on TV.

The schedule listed Cavaliers games on national television 13 times, remarkable for a team following up a last-place finish.

BLENDING WITH THE GUYS

One of James's most admirable attributes as a young player, even as people wrote and talked about how great he was and how great he was going to be, was his aggressiveness toward working on his game. After sampling some NBA level competition, James realized he had to improve the accuracy of his outside shot. In high school, he was stronger and quicker than most opponents and could drive to the basket and dunk over them, almost at will. In the NBA he would become a more dangerous offensive weapon by expanding his shooting range. Similarly, in the summer league, when he played the point, James ran across some guards who were faster than he was and challenged his defensive skills.

It is a long-held tradition in professional sports that rookies, no matter how heralded or important to the success of the team, are treated as rookies. They are humbled by the veterans and made to perform menial tasks, to help with minor chores, and sometimes sing their college fight songs. The newcomers may be millionaires and the future of the team may be riding on them on the field and at the bank, but rookie razzing is one minor way to keep those players grounded. One practical joke became very public when Cavaliers vets orchestrated a scene where James and fellow rookie Jason Kapono were told to run out onto the court first at the start of an exhibition game. The players dashed onto the floor, only to discover their teammates failed to follow. They floundered around alone on the floor in front of the crowd wondering what happened to everyone else. The other Cavaliers had a good giggle.

James also revealed that his teammates decided it was his responsibility to bring the Krispy Kreme doughnuts to practice every day (he could afford it) and in another time-honored rookie tradition, they forced him to carry their luggage in hotels and to the bus while on road trips. Once in a great while, prima donna rookies try to shun the role because their egos can't handle being treated like bell boys. Recognizing it was important, with all of the attention he garnered, not to come off as spoiled, James good naturedly played along and avoided bucking the system. The Cavaliers knew, he said, that he was not trying to usurp locker room authority.

James remained self-effacing in press conferences, telling the hordes of reporters who turned up for practice that he was not the big man on the team. He pointed to the top returning veterans, singling out guard Ricky

Davis, a potent outside shooter, and 7-foot-3 center Zydrunas Ilgauskus. The acquisition of the big Lithuanian was touted as a major coup for the Cavs in 1996, but he seemed jinxed. Ilgauskus averaged a useful 15 points a game when he was healthy. The problem was that the big guy missed two complete seasons and parts of others with injuries. His feet were particularly fragile and at times it was suggested he might have to retire young.

These were gracious comments from James—and wise ones from a spectacularly hyped rookie trying to make friends with and mesh with teammates—but everyone knew that James had been brought in to be The Man. After all, the others collectively had failed dramatically the year before. There was no harm in being polite, though, and in stroking other egos as well. During training camp, James, as he had been so often elsewhere, was the main focus of attention from the media. He would not have been worth his salt as a confident professional athlete if he had not said it, but some eyes rolled when James predicted that the rejuvenated Cavaliers should make the playoffs.

James's comments might have been a subtle challenge to his teammates. If so, that was a sign of leadership that James's coaches and bosses could appreciate. Rome wasn't built in a day and neither was any professional sports team. The building blocks for both had to be in place and the hands of craftsmanship at the controls, but these things took time. As befitting what they hoped would be a new era with LeBron James, the Cavaliers designed and unveiled flashy new uniform jerseys. They were splendid in burgundy and gold and they were striking in white with burgundy trim.

When he was still in high school, reporters making James's acquaintance for the first time often gushed about how mature beyond his years he seemed. Now traveling in the adult world, the same observations were generally made. Still, once in a while James let some of the "gee-whiz" nature of his personality come out. He seemed more like a high schooler for a minute when the Cavaliers met the Los Angeles Lakers of Shaquille O'Neal, Kobe Bryant, and Gary Payton in an exhibition game and he said, "Last year I was just watching them every night on TV."[3] And now he was trying to outplay them.

The NBA exhibition season is about tuning up for the regular season. It allows coaches to experiment with lineups and decide who should be starting and who should be playing what role. It provides fringe players with the chance to make the 12-man active roster. It allows rookies to gain game experience. Wins and losses are virtually irrelevant. At the end of training camp Silas named James as one of his starters. The coach decided against starting James at point guard and put him at his most natural position of small forward, or scoring forward.

The day before the Cavaliers were scheduled to start the season, James had lunch with Moses Malone, the first truly successful player to jump right from high school play to the pros. Although 30 years had passed, Malone realized James would face some of the same challenges he took on. Malone wasn't worried about James's talent. He wanted to proffer advice on day-to-day NBA living.

James shrugged off any pressure in his debut. He was subdued because the Cavaliers lost, but in becoming the first player to score as many as 20 points and record 9 assists in his first game in 22 years, or since Isiah Thomas did it with the Detroit Pistons, James had proven himself ready for NBA competition.

INSTANT IMPACT

Every team in the NBA hopes that its No. 1 draft pick is good enough to start and contribute. It doesn't always work that way. But the No. 1 pick overall in the draft should be ready to go. LeBron James was ready, but in his first several games in Cleveland's lineup, it was not immediately apparent that the Cavaliers were.

It took six tries for the Cavaliers to win a game. They were 0–5 when they finally bested the Washington Wizards, 111–98, during James's rookie year. James turned in a box score line that was every bit as diversified as the ones he recorded for St. Vincent-St. Mary. He scored 17 points and added 9 assists and 8 rebounds.

Eyes from many walks of life were on James, not just the basketball world. From the moment he signed his huge Nike contract and followed it up with deals for other products, marketing and business experts debated whether James was worth it. Rick Burton, executive director of the Warsaw Sports Marketing Center at the University of Oregon, compared James to the movie character Neo played by Keanu Reeves in "The Matrix." "There are a bunch of people who think he is 'The One,'" Burton said. "They think he will lead them back to that time when there was that dominating player that the whole league revolved around."[4] It was clear that basketball people had already anointed James with that cache since he had been carrying around the nickname "The Chosen One" for two years by that point.

Regardless of a player's talent, the move to professional sports, blending with a team at the highest level of play, is going to involve some glitches. James was not going to be perfect every game. He was not going to lead his team—a weak one at that—to victory every night. To a degree, he was going to be a work in progress his entire rookie year, with flashes of brilliance, games of competence, and days when things didn't go right. Even the best athletes in every sport who play long seasons have off days. It was bound to happen to James and it did.

As usual, media patience was in short supply. Depending on the game, sports reporters either praised James to the heavens or suggested he had much to learn. Mostly, those were snapshot observations, cases of checking in on James for one night's play. Newspaper critics said James was not as good as advertised. Those who took a step back and watched James in more than one game and recognized the pressures and attention focused on him offered more level-headed appraisals. Before a Cavaliers-Chicago Bulls game in mid-December of James's rookie year, it was noted, "If you want to see a remarkably mature rookie laboring with a bad team under unreasonable and unyielding expectations, then James is the ticket. He is a young man destined to be very good with a sophisticated all-around game."[5]

If fans were disappointed that James did not slam down a flashy enough dunk to make it onto the ESPN Sports Center highlights every night, it was their own fault for expecting it. James was doing what he always had. He was playing basketball the way he had been taught. He was never a ball hog. He rarely scored on designed spectacular moves, but rather made spectacular moves to avoid the defense. He still passed up shots to feed teammates on the Cavaliers the same way he had with the Fighting Irish. James was just being himself and those who knew the sport best realized it and marveled at it.

NOT MUCH LEARNING CURVE

"He thinks the game better than anyone his age," Bulls general manager John Paxson said. "You watch him and the first thing you notice is how unselfish he is. Every kid who comes into this league wants to score. The only thing they know is to play with the ball in their hands. They don't care about getting others involved. With this kid, that's his first thought. He's not given enough credit for that."[6]

Attracting nearly as much scrutiny was James's old friend Carmelo Anthony, who was drafted by the Denver Nuggets. They were being hailed as the game's great new twosome, the most significant linked new faces since Larry Bird of the Celtics and Magic Johnson of the Lakers showed up to pump up a fresh team rivalry nearly 25 years earlier. Every athlete needs a foil. It's good for business when rivalries generate emotion and competition. The James-Anthony rivalry would be limited—at least for the present—because the two stars played in different divisions and would play few regular-season games against one another. When their teams advanced to the playoffs they would be on opposite sides of the bracket, too, so they could only meet in the finals. Those days were expected to be far in the future for both clubs still reeling from their 15–67 records of the year before.

Every professional basketball player was a star somewhere along the line, usually in high school or college, or in a foreign league if they are from overseas. Chances are they were the best somewhere and when they reached the NBA they still expected to be the best. Reality sets in abruptly or gradually. A player might find he is lucky to make the 12-man active roster. A player might find he is lucky to be one of the five starters. But there are only about 25 all-stars and barely more than a handful of superstars. From the beginning of James's NBA career, other players recognized that he was going to be one of those superstars. Part of the reason was his raw talent. Part of it was his demeanor and work ethic. And part of it was that until December 30 of his rookie year, he was still 18 years old. For the second half of his debut season, James was all of 19.

"He is a complete basketball player," said Avery Johnson, then a veteran guard with the Golden State Warriors who became coach of the Dallas Mavericks. "He can do things that you just cannot teach. When I was 19 years old, I was just trying to pass a geometry class in college."[7]

The most complex geometry problem that James would have faced that year was the triangle offense. But his team didn't use it. That offensive set was not in Coach Paul Silas's bag of tricks. Silas, however, was the man who most closely watched James day-to-day in practice and in games, judging his effectiveness, his hustle, his fatigue, and his defensive capabilities. Silas saw the future and made a breathtaking prediction. In all of NBA history, only one player has averaged in double digits in points, rebounds, and assists for an entire season. That was Hall of Fame guard Oscar Robertson, who in his prime during the 1960s may have been the best player who ever lived. Halfway through James's rookie season, Silas uttered his brash statement. "Eventually, I think he can average a triple double," Silas said. "He's 6–8, so he should rebound. But 10 rebounds is not out of the question. He's going to have the ball, so 10 assists isn't out of the question. And he's going to score in double figures."[8] Silas made the observation so casually, so routinely, that it did not receive inordinate attention. Not only was Robertson the only player to accomplish the feat, no other coach was on record talking about any player suggesting that another star would pull it off.

By the time James made a circuit around the league, opposing coaches and players who had not studied up on his high school career had become true believers, and they were not just talking about pure basketball prowess. They could see that he possessed innate court vision and they could see why corporations wanted to attach their names to his. "Go beyond the individual, the guy has it," then-Houston Rockets Coach Jeff Van Gundy said. "He has it. He's got poise. He's got presence. He's got vision. He's got command of his game. He's one of those guys who's just an intelligent basketball player, on top of being a superior talent. So, what do you have? You've got greatness."[9]

MAKING IT INTO LEBRON'S TEAM

In mid-December, the Cavaliers traded guard Ricky Davis, one of their high scorers, to Boston in a six-man deal that also involved a draft pick. In a sense this was a vote of confidence in James's offensive skills. It was time, Silas and the team was saying, for him to score more. Whether it was the prod from management or the fact that there were more opportunities to shoot with Davis gone, James immediately became a scoring machine. He scored 36 points in an 88–81 victory at Philadelphia on December 19. He scored 32 points with 10 assists in a 95–87 victory at Chicago. He scored 34 points in a 113–101 overtime loss to Orlando on Christmas Day. Traditionally, the NBA schedules only prime-time teams for its Christmas extravaganza. The Cavaliers had not been televised on Christmas in 14 years. On December 28, James scored 32 points and added 10 rebounds and 9 assists in an 86–74 victory over Portland.

Some NBA players were only vaguely aware of James's high school exploits and heard more about his problems surrounding Hummergate and Jerseygate. They didn't know what type of guy he was and wondered if he would be haughty because of all the advance attention. Teammate Ira Newbie, a much less publicized 6-foot-7 forward, was impressed by James's sincerity. "LeBron just wants to fit in and contribute, basically give his heart to win," Newbie said. "It's completely genuine."[10]

As much as the NBA relies on big-name stars to sell its product to the public, it is common knowledge that superstars need strong supporting casts to make the playoffs and win championships. Michael Jordan was a super player for the Chicago Bulls for several years before he became a super winner. Bulls management had to build a good team around him. At the height of his fame, some made fun of the other Bulls as "The Jordanaires," suggesting it didn't really matter who the other four players were on the floor with Jordan. But it did. B. J. Armstrong, a guard on some of the Bulls' title teams, said very few players can single handedly improve a team by as much as 10 games in the standings: "That's the barometer in this league."[11] The Cavaliers' win-loss record improved by 18 games during James's rookie year.

James continued to excel as a rookie and sometimes crossed over to the spectacular. He scored 38 points in a Cavs win over Washington on February 1, and 32 points in a win over the San Antonio Spurs on February 20. It surprised many fans when neither James nor Carmelo Anthony was selected to play in the annual mid-season All-Star game. James was averaging 21 points per game at the time and Anthony was right behind him at 19 points per game. Instead, they were both invited to play in the Rookie Challenge game against a team of NBA second-year men. That was not the main stage, but at least it involved them in the festivities. James scored 33 points in the rookie game.

Under the direction of Silas, LeBron James and the Cavaliers were actually steadily improving. James had pledged to bring Cleveland into the playoffs, and for the last month of the regular season, the Cavs contended for the eighth playoff spot in the Eastern Conference. But the Cavaliers had dug themselves a hole with their 6–19 start, so while hope beat in the breast of long-disappointed Cavaliers' fans, the odds were still against Cleveland making the leap from last to the playoffs.

Even Silas was pleasantly surprised. "No, I didn't expect to be where we are now," he said. "There's no way I thought we'd be anywhere in the hunt now."[12]

A new measure of James's popularity popped up in popular culture. For a March 3, 2004 game against the Atlanta Hawks at Gund Arena, the Cavaliers gave away thousands of LeBron James bobble-head dolls, replicas of the player standing 7 1/2 inches tall. Players and even Coach Silas scooped them up as souvenirs. In the current sports marketplace, that is a prized item. Milking every moment of the occasion for fun-and-games publicity, the Cavaliers had the bobble heads delivered to the arena by armored truck and assigned team mascot "Moondog" as one of the security guards to accompany the mini-statues into the building. They were as hot as Beanie Babies or any other collectible oddity.

During the ensuing stretch of March, as they galloped toward what they hoped would be a playoff reward, the Cavs won seven games in a row. James's 41 points on March 27 keyed a 107–103 victory over the New Jersey Nets.

Winning more games featuring one of the most charismatic players in the league and putting together a run at a playoff position was refreshing for Cavaliers fans and paid off at the box office. During the depressing 2002–03 season, pre-LeBron, the Cavaliers averaged 11,497 fans per game at Gund Arena. The next season, James's rookie year, the Cavaliers averaged 18,288 fans per home game. In 20 years in Richfield, the Cavs averaged better than that twice, and in both instances, by less than 100

fans per game. Only the 1994–95 first season played at Gund, exceeded the
Cleveland average for a single season with 20,338 spectators per game.

"I can remember coming in here when there were 5,000 at the most,"
Silas said of his coaching days with the Hornets. "That (the new crowds)
is exciting and it just shows you the fans like to see good basketball. I
think we're beginning to provide that."[13]

The Cavaliers could not maintain their steam and did not qualify for
the playoffs James's rookie year. They finished 35–47, a record that did not
strike fear into the hearts of the league's best teams, but did instill a sense
of optimism in Cleveland's devoted fans. They could see better times on
the horizon. James averaged 20.9 points per game as a rookie and contributed 5.5 rebounds and 5.9 assists. He was voted NBA rookie-of-the-year,
becoming the first from the Cavaliers selected for the honor. And at 19,
James was the youngest player ever to win.

The award winner was announced about a week after the Cavaliers'
season ended and in one of his few faux pas of the season, James was 45
minutes late to the press conference. He tried to make light of it, saying
he was so tired from the season he didn't want to get out of bed.

The long-awaited LeBron James rookie season was officially over. The
long-awaited rest of his basketball career was just beginning.

NOTES

1. Roger Gordon, *The Rookie Season of LeBron James* (Champaign, Ill., Sports
Publishing LLC, 2004) p. 83.

2. B. J. Robinson, *LeBron James—King of the Court* (East Cleveland, Forest
Hill Publishing LLC, 2005) p. 140.

3. Robinson, p. 152.

4. Ralph Frammolino, *Los Angeles Times*, May 23, 2003.

5. Sam Smith, *Chicago Tribune*, December 19, 2003.

6. Smith, *Chicago Tribune*.

7. Gordon, p. 18.

8. Smith, *Chicago Tribune*.

9. Gordon, p. 39.

10. Gordon, p. 50.

11. Robinson, p. 15.

12. Sam Smith, *Chicago Tribune*, March 1, 2004.

13. K. C. Johnson, *Chicago Tribune*, December 27, 2003.

LeBron James as a high school star for St. Vincent-St. Mary's of Akron, running downcourt in one of the biggest games of his high school career for the Irish against Oak Hill Academy of Virginia in a clash of nationally rated schools, Dec. 12, 2002. James's team won 65–45. AP Photo/Mark Duncan.

Gloria James, who raised LeBron as a single mother, wearing a jersey representing her son's high school team and holding up ping-pong paddles with his face superimposed at an intersectional game in Greensboro, N.C., Jan. 20, 2003, against Reynolds High School. AP Photo/Chuck Burton.

Representing his country, LeBron James makes a flashy shot for the United States in the team's bronze medal victory over Argentina in September 2006 in Japan. He is scoring over Luis Scola. AP Photo/ Dusan Vranic.

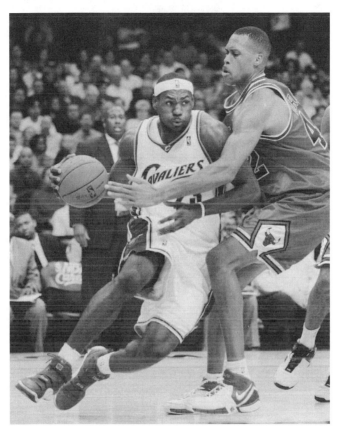

Explosive scorer LeBron James drives to the basket in a November 9, 2006 game against the Chicago Bulls as Bulls forward P. J. Brown commits a foul while trying to stop him. AP Photo/Mark Duncan.

LeBron James (left) and teammate Drew Gooden watch James's son LeBron Jr. dance to arena music during a timeout of a 90–68 blowout triumph over the New York Knicks on March 23, 2007. AP Photo/Tony Dejak.

Chapter 7

RED, WHITE, AND BLUE

For decades, Americans dominated Olympic basketball. All it took for the United States to win the gold medal was to show up. Basketball is an American game, invented in the United States in Springfield, Massachusetts, and it seemed as if the U.S. men's team in the Summer Games had a divine right to the gold.

By the end of the 1990s, however, the rest of the world showed signs of catching up. Games in international play were closer. U.S. representatives began losing games, then losing the gold. By the time the Olympics in Athens, Greece turned up on the schedule in the summer of 2004, rather than being universally praised as the best team in the world, the domestic hoopsters were the object of queries such as, "What's wrong with the Americans?" Where once it was believed that any thrown-together team of U.S. amateurs could conquer the world, it was well known that not even a squad of the best American professionals had a lock on the gold medal. Committees representing USA Basketball met for hours debating the type of coaches and players to choose to represent the country. They performed these services well aware that they would be scrutinized by dissatisfied and disappointed American basketball fans who had not yet grasped the situation about the depth of talent being produced by other nations. They still felt that the gold was their birthright in this sport.

Soon after LeBron James's rookie season with the Cavaliers concluded, James was issued an invitation to join the U.S. Olympic team for the games in Greece. It was an honor to be selected and for the first time in his basketball career, the placement of James on a basketball team did not guarantee playing time. He was joining up with a full roster of older players with more experience who had been around the NBA. James was still 19 and the youngest player on the team. For the first time in years, since his freshman season at St. Vincent-St. Mary, James was assigned a different uniform number than his traditional 23. In the Games, James wore No. 6. When the U.S. team roster was solidified in mid-summer, Carmelo Anthony became a squad member, too. They represented the young guns whose NBA careers were just beginning.

This was an American all-star team and members of the squad were NBA all-stars. Among the other U.S. players were Tim Duncan, Allen Iverson, Shawn Marion, Stephon Marbury, and Amare Stoudemire. Dwayne Wade, the former Marquette star who was a member of the same NBA rookie class as James and Anthony, and who startled fans with his sterling play, was also an Olympian. Was this the absolute finest American team that could be put together? No. Some pros opted out of playing for a variety of personal reasons. This was a new look for the United States, relying mostly on young players on the cusp of superstardom, and trying to mesh a unit that could contend with and defeat teams from other nations that had shared the court together for years.

The man who was handed the reins to this youthful team was Coach Larry Brown. Brown was coming off a season where he had led the Detroit Pistons to the NBA title. He has long been highly regarded as a teacher of the sport, but he is also regarded as a coach who can be hard on his players. One question was whether Brown and his players could get along well enough to bring home the spoils. Could the players brush off Brown's sharp comments to perform? Could Brown overlook the frequent mistakes a young team would make? James, for one, was constantly asked about being the youngest member of the team. "I'm still young," he said, "but I've learned so much in the 19 years I've been alive. I'm a teenager in age, but I've been a man a long time."[1]

The United States—the team and the fans—found out early that this was not going to be one of the country's old-fashioned cruises to the gold that so many in the basketball world were used to seeing. The Americans were thumped, unexpectedly, by a solid Puerto Rican team, 92–73. It was the United States' first loss in 25 Olympic contests. The defeat was a shock and it exposed weaknesses Americans felt had been overcome by the choice of players and the Larry Brown drills. The United States shot poorly, especially from the three-point arc, and did not jell as a team. The game was a portent of a very frustrating, disappointing Olympic experience for Brown, the players, and the United States.

After the stunning loss, the United States bested Greece and Australia, but fell to Lithuania, before topping Angola. The Americans then deposited a key victory over Spain in the win column, setting up a semifinal match with Argentina. A win would have kept the United States alive for a gold medal, despite early erratic play, but the Americans lost by eight points. In a society where a gold-medal performance was really the only acceptable result, the United States was out of the picture before the final game. The team rallied and scored the bronze medal by taking out Lithuania in a rematch to avoid going home empty-handed. But bronze medals in Olympic basketball are more frustrating consolation prize than achievement in the United States. Rather than be applauded for winning a medal, the Americans, who fell short of their own expectations, were quizzed on why they "failed."

VIEW FROM THE BENCH

For the first time in his life, LeBron James was a non-factor on a basketball team and was used only selectively. He spent most of the U.S. games hanging out at the end of the bench shooting the breeze with Anthony and cheering for teammates on the court. Frequently, James's line-score contributions were summed up in single digits for minutes played and in single digits for points scored. Once in a while he broke loose, contributing 11 points in the Angola victory. He also scored 10 points against Greece.

James had opportunities to criticize the way he was used in the games, but took the high road and didn't complain. He was gracious and told reporters he was proud to represent his country, and that he was learning from the experience of being on the U.S. team.

It was an unusual situation for James. He was making news by not playing. He didn't want to make more news by opening his mouth and saying something regrettable. As it was, USA Basketball men's selection committee chairman Stu Jackson said after the Athens Games that James might be a prospect for two or three more U.S. Olympic teams.

By the next season, James was definitely thinking ahead to the 2008 Olympics in Beijing—he was taking Chinese lessons. When a film crew from China interviewed him in the Cavs' locker room in late 2006, James said, "Nee-how," or hello, in Chinese, on camera.[2]

When it comes to LeBron James, the public appetite for news, gossip, or off-beat developments never ceases. A full-fledged professional, with earning power stretching in all directions after signing his megabucks endorsement contracts with Nike, Coca-Cola, and beyond, James found that his Olympic experience was bracketed by breathless breaking reports that indicated he had become an "A" list celebrity whose every move was monitored.

SELLING LEBRON

In late July 2004, a sports trading card that featured James and his idol, Michael Jordan, printed by Upper Deck, sold on eBay for $150,000. That was the highest price ever paid for a card printed since 1980 representing any sport. The single most valuable sports card is a rare Honus Wagner baseball card from 1906 that has sold for more than $2 million. The price paid for the James-Jordan card stunned many because the card was manufactured in 2004. Cloth NBA logo swatches were imbedded into the card, driving up its value. A James-Kobe Bryant card of similar rarity sold for $62,100 before the James-Jordan card hit the market.[3]

Not to be outflanked in the popular culture wars, about a month later, Coca-Cola announced a deal with DC Comics (producers of Superman and Batman comic books for decades) to print a LeBron James comic book used as a vehicle to promote Powerade Falva23, a new sports drink that James had input into inventing. The color was described as burgundy and the flavor as "sourberry." After the player saw the art work for the adventures of LeBron James, he asked to be depicted with larger muscles. Then he got behind the effort that was scheduled for a 3-million magazine print run. "I mean, ripped muscles, impossible moves, scoring at will, and beating the bad guys, who wouldn't want to be a heroic basketball player in a comic book?" James said.[4]

James had always been a fan of comic books, so it was a special treat to be featured in one. Likewise, he had always been a fan of chewing gum. His newest endorsement deal was a commitment to work with Bubblicious gum and James got the chance to have his own brand called "Lightning Lemonade."

True to his word when he turned pro, James was still having fun.

Then things got more serious, although the event was a joyous one. James's longtime girlfriend Savannah Brinson, gave birth to his first child, LeBron James Jr. The young man who had grown up without knowing his genetic father and who had been mostly raised by single mother Gloria, was very thoughtful about this new addition to his life. The baby was born on October 6, 2004, and James said he was humbled by his new role of fatherhood and the responsibilities he knew it entailed. "It's really calmed me down by being a father now," James said on the cusp of his second NBA season. "It keeps me grounded. I got to represent for my whole family now. I can't, in no way, shape or form try to hurt my name."[5]

The man who seemed to have everything from riches and fame to a good life served on the platter of professional sports talked about being humbled in two ways—not playing much in the Olympics and being a new dad. But he was still the same old LeBron in many ways. He watched long hours of film to study his moves and improve his basketball skills. James rode a bicycle for long hours to improve his stamina. He had learned so much, paid many hardscrabble dues, but James was always the first to say that he could get better. And it was his goal to show it to the world during his second campaign with the Cleveland Cavaliers.

CLEVELAND PART II

When LeBron James's second season with the Cavaliers began, it was apparent that all of the talk he made about practicing and working on his game was not merely lip service. He wasn't just uttering those statements because they were politically correct, but because they reflected his beliefs. It was easy to discern that he was telling the truth, because the Cavaliers realized they had a new, improved LeBron. He was a better player than he was as a rookie and there weren't too many complaints about James's performance in his first season. If there was a gripe at all, it was that James shot only 41.7 percent from the field his first year. Basketball people said he must do better and James acknowledged that he wanted to do better, pushing his shooting accuracy nearer to 50 percent.

Almost immediately, it was clear in the fall of 2004 that not only was James a better player his second time around the NBA, but the Cavaliers were a better team. With each early-season victory, a genuine sense of fan excitement grew from a feeling of "One day LeBron James will lead us through a special season" to "LeBron might be able to take us someplace special right now."

After James redoubled his efforts to make his jump shot sharper and to work harder on his one-on-one defense, he sounded uncharacteristically outspoken at the beginning of the Cavs' 2004–05 season. "It's going to be a breeze for me," he said.[6] Maybe a breeze was an overstatement because no one questioned how hard James sweated (he really needed his trademark headband to keep the perspiration out of his eyes), but less than two months into the new season James was shooting 49.3 percent from the floor. The Cavaliers had also posted a record of 14–9. It was nearly four years since Cleveland had been over .500 in the standings.

James was complimented so much when he was in high school that it would have been easy for him to blow off extra workouts and arrive in the

NBA ill-prepared. The history of some high school players looking lost on the court as rookies made some basketball experts reserve judgment on James before his rookie-of-the-year season. Once again James could have rested on his laurels, but instead he returned for his second season ready to move into the top echelon of league stars.

No one appreciated the new-look LeBron more than his coaches and teammates. They practiced with him every day, watched him closely during games, and could make easy comparisons in his play from one year to the next. Coach Paul Silas marveled at the differences he saw in James's capabilities over a short time. "I have never seen a player learn so much in one year," Silas said of his star. "He is further ahead than I thought he would be at this time. He's so much more aware, so much better than he was last year as a rookie."[7]

When James first joined the Cavaliers, he was careful not to insult veterans and step into their leadership territory. He was physically their equal with his perfect forward height of 6-foot-8 and his hefty power build of 240 pounds. James was rated a special talent, however, because he was faster than most other players, especially on his first step to the basket to drive for a lay-up, and he could out-jump most. In his second season, James was no longer verbally reticent. He realized he was being looked to as the team leader and although he did not turn 20 years old until the season was about eight weeks old, he felt it was his responsibility to carry the franchise to the next level of improvement. To James, the dream reward for a last-place team of two seasons earlier was defined as carrying the Cavs into the postseason. To him it was playoffs or bust. And he wasn't shy about stating that aspiration at the start of the season.

GETTING BETTER ALL THE TIME

James began running up higher point totals in the Cavs' games and he gained more admirers. He raised his points per game to more than 27 and that propelled him into the league's top five. When James scored 43 points in an early-season Cleveland triumph over Larry Brown's Detroit Pistons, it was speculated that James might have been out for revenge for his Olympic benching.

James never said a word about showing Brown a thing or two, but if he played extra hard to prove a point that would not have been surprising and it would have paralleled the oft-reported behavior of his hero Michael Jordan. Jordan regularly used slights—real or imagined—for motivation when playing selected teams. Still, Brown had taken the time to mail James a congratulatory present for his newborn son only a month or so earlier, and James hand-delivered a thank-you card to Brown before the start of the game. The two acts of consideration implied that there was no game of one-upmanship involved when the Pistons and Cavaliers met, although from the outside James's big night could be interpreted as a vengeance performance.

Major league baseball is the king of all sports when it comes to keeping track of statistics and numbers for its games dating back to the nineteenth century. No other sport is as comprehensive. More arcane baseball records are at historians' and reporters' fingertips than in any other sport. Over the last three decades, however, basketball has become much more efficient in tallying records of different sorts and in monitoring statistics such as triple-doubles and blocked shots that once were of no consequence to the NBA hierarchy. Some of this fastidiousness affected James.

He celebrated his 20th birthday on December 30, 2004, and that plunged researchers into a records search for a mark that had not been long in the making. It was determined that James's 2,362 points made him the most prolific scoring teenager in NBA history. He was 503 points ahead of Kobe Bryant. It is not a statistic that will be remembered by the casual fan the way the breaking of a baseball home run record is, but it did put in perspective that James had accomplished much professionally at an early age. For one thing, his maturity at a young age meant that his team did not worry about giving him more playing time as an 18- and 19-year-old than Bryant, Kevin Garnett, and Tracy McGrady. Time on the court led to shots through the hoop.

Complicating James's swift second-year start, however, was an injury. When he collapsed to the floor during a December 19 game against the Houston Rockets, it was not immediately obvious how severely hurt he was. Dikembe Mutombo, one of the NBA's top defensive centers, has always been very protective of the ball when he rebounds. He swung an elbow and caught James in the face. The force of the blow knocked James to the floor and he suffered a broken cheekbone. James did not permit the injury to interrupt his hot streak. When he returned to the lineup a couple of days later for a game against Charlotte, he wore a protective mask. James also scored 26 points. The incident, James's reaction to it, and his response—returning quickly to play wearing an uncomfortable, awkward looking protective device to shield his face—became another measuring stick among NBA players. Some players are ridiculed for begging off game action with injuries that others consider insignificant. Other players gain admiration for their toughness by "playing with pain," as the phrase is used in conversation and among TV play-by-by broadcasters.

The mask was a nuisance, because it somewhat limited James's vision, but he shrugged off the inconvenience and did not let the obstacle interfere with his play. During a victory over Portland about a month after adapting to the mask, James turned in a triple double of 27 points, 11 rebounds, and 10 assists.

NEW BOSSES

Early in that season, major changes came to the Cavaliers' front office. Gordon Gund sold his stake in the team and the club brought a new owner, Dan Gilbert, into the NBA ruling brotherhood with the $375 million purchase. Gilbert operated a company called Quicken Loans and soon enough the name of the home arena of the Cavaliers was changed to Quicken Loans Arena, although many called it "The Q." Coach Paul Silas was dismissed and interim coach Brendan Malone took over the team for the rest of the season.

James was not selected for the NBA All-Star game as a rookie and had to be content competing in the rookie challenge against second-year players. During his second year, however, James was too good to relegate to that lesser show in the double feature. As a sophomore, James was invited to the Big Show. He was one of seven first-time all-stars in the game that season, provoking discussion about a changing of the guard among the sport's top players, and whether James in this particular all-star celebration was actually experiencing a coronation as the real King James. When asked if he was being passed the torch as superstar of the league, James said, "Will there be resentment? I don't know. It's something that's been going on since I was a sophomore in high school."[8]

A month after the All-Star game, James knocked down a career-high 56 points while shooting 18-of-36 from the field and 14-of-15 from the free-throw line, although the Cavaliers lost the game to the Toronto Raptors. The achievement made him the youngest player in NBA history to score 50 points in a game. A month later, James and others were caught off guard when *Time Magazine* named him one of the 100 most influential people in the world. Not the basketball world, but the entire world—politicians, economists, novelists included. There were only four other sports figures mentioned on the list—Richard Pound, head of the World Anti-Doping Agency, solo around-the-world sailor Ellen MacArthur, auto racing star Michael Shumacher, and Roman Abramovich, owner of the English soccer club Chelsea.[9]

On the basketball court, James indeed leaped into the rankings of the top five players in the league. His individual brilliance showed game by game, and he uplifted the Cavaliers in the standings. Coming close to his preseason prediction, Cleveland was in the hunt for a playoff spot until the last days of the season. The Cavs' regular-season record was 42–40, the team's first winning mark since the 1997–98 season, and they came within a single win of what James had projected as minimally acceptable to him. The season mark was the eighth best record in the Eastern Conference and ordinarily would have given the Cavs the playoff spot they hungered for, but the New Jersey Nets earned the berth based on tiebreakers.

The Cavaliers made noise around the league. They were viewed as a much more dangerous opponent than they had been two seasons earlier, and hometown fans recognized the changes and showed approval with their ticket-buying habits, contributing to a season attendance average of 19,128. All of the good numbers were on the rise for Cleveland, from wins to spectators—and for James, too. During his second NBA season, James averaged 27.2 points a game, third best in the league, 7.7 rebounds, and 7.2 assists. He also used his quickness to make more than two steals per game. In every measurable way during the 2004–05 season, James and the Cavaliers were better. No longer would anyone scoff if LeBron James mentioned the words "playoffs" and "Cavaliers" in the same sentence. The player and his team had displayed enough for everyone to realize it was not wishful thinking, but almost certainly a foregone conclusion for 2005–06.

NOTES

1. B. J. Robinson, *LeBron James—King of the Court* (East Cleveland: Forest Hills Publishing, 2005), p. 171.

2. LeBron James, pre-game press conference, Quicken Loans Arena, November 9, 2006.

3. *Chicago Tribune* Redeye edition, July 26, 2004.

4. *Chicago Tribune*, August 20, 2004.

5. Robinson, p. 179.

6. Sean Deveney, *The Sporting News*, December 16, 2004.

7. Deveney, *The Sporting News*.

8. Sam Smith, *Chicago Tribune*, February 20, 2005.

9. *Time Magazine*, April 11, 2005.

Chapter 8

JUNIOR YEAR PRO

One man does not make a championship team, no matter how talented he is. But one man can uplift a team, and entering the 2005–06 season it was unclear whether LeBron James was going to be a one-man Cavaliers club or whether the construction of a team around him was paying off.

Skeptical basketball observers still felt that Cleveland was a one-man team, not a team ready for the playoffs or to make a run for Eastern Conference supremacy. James thought differently. Once again he believed he was improved and so were the Cavs. And once again he set out to prove it.

During the summer leading into his third season, James flexed his muscles verbally. At the start of the NBA's annual free-agent season, he publicly urged the Cavaliers to be aggressive in seeking new faces and said he would like his opinions to be considered when the team went after guys through trades or free-agent signings. At the time, such luminaries and potentially helpful players as guards Ray Allen, Larry Hughes, and Michael Redd appeared available. The Cavs did sign Hughes, previously of the Washington Wizards, hoping he could be a scoring point guard and might work well with James.[1] Despite some injuries, Hughes did play a critical role with the Cavaliers once he joined the team. And Cleveland also added forward Donyell Marshall, who left the Toronto Raptors.

Later that summer the impact of some of James's endorsement deals also went public when his face, drawn in a cartoon-like fashion, was imprinted on NASCAR driver Bobby Labonte's hood for a race. It was part of James's connection to Powerade through his Coca-Cola contract. If anybody in North Carolina had not known about James before, they did then.

James also poured himself into charitable efforts before Cavs train-ing camp, instituting a "LeBron's King for Kids Bike-A-Thon" in Akron; and after Hurricane Katrina struck New Orleans and the Mississippi Gulf Coast, he contributed his own labor to the relief work. James worked with teams of people to load food, school supplies, and diapers onto trucks bound for the South.

Cleveland fans lauded James's public service efforts, but they worried in October when he became sick and was hospitalized. The incident oc-curred during Cavs training camp. James felt ill during practice. When team doctors examined him it was originally believed that James suffered a minor strain of a pectoral muscle. Upon further review, however, it was determined that James had been struck by pleurisy, affecting his lungs and chest. After Cavalier supporters passed through a short period of dread and alarm, James resumed practicing and returned to full strength.

SCORING MORE THAN EVER

Once the games began for real, James resumed doing what he does best, scoring points and leading his team. About two weeks into the season, James passed another milestone, although somewhat of an arcane one that simply reinforced that he was accomplishing more at a younger age than any previous NBA player. In a triumph over the Orlando Magic, James became the youngest performer to record 4,000 points in his career. He was 20 years and 318 days old, and he broke the record set previously by Kobe Bryant, who was 21 years and 216 days old when he established the old mark. "Unbelievable," commented Cavs coach Mike Brown, who had replaced Paul Silas, after serving as an assistant coach with the Indi-ana Pacers and the San Antonio Spurs. "That kid is a talent. It couldn't happen to a better person. He's a great person, a great leader and I enjoy being around him. To be around him when it happened is a tremendous feeling."[2]

The mini-milestone was insignificant, however, compared to how the Cavaliers were playing. They were starting to act like grownups, begin-ning to jell as the improving team James had promised. During a De-cember showdown with the equally young and promising Chicago Bulls, James was the difference maker. He scored 37 points to propel Cleveland over Chicago, 108–100, and that was at the United Center, the Bulls' home court, a difficult place to win. "We're becoming a great team," James said. "Right now we're a good team. I feel like we're getting there to be one of the best teams in the Eastern Conference."[3] The Eastern Conference was in the midst of a lull between great teams. The Western

Conference housed most of the best teams in the NBA at the time. There was a vacuum in power at the top of the East and if James's projections were correct, the Cavs had just as good a chance to fill it as teams like Chicago and Detroit.

As the calendar year came to an end, James turned 21. The toast of Cleveland was thrown a glitzy, invitation-only party two days before December 30, where entry fees of $50 to $300 were charged at Cleveland's House of Blues and some of the proceeds were given to charity. James, who had made a splash nationally when he received his first car, that old Hummer, arrived at the party in a new vehicle, a black Rolls Royce. In contrast to the car, James wore a white suit, a look he had already displayed on draft day. The question of what to buy for the man who has everything recurred many times. After all, James had the money to purchase anything he wanted. One of the revelers was Cavs coach Mike Brown, and when he was asked about the gift problem he said he had referred the issue to his wife Carolyn. "What do you get LeBron?" Brown said she asked. "I don't know, babe," Brown said he told her. "You can figure it out."[4]

Left unsaid was that the most satisfying present anyone could give to James was a world championship. But such gifts do not change hands at parties, and if James was going to be the recipient of such a prized present, he was going to have to work for it.

James's face and persona were becoming more widespread in the marketing world as he continued to light up NBA scoreboards. At sports memorabilia shows, James bobble-heads and framed photographs proliferated. Stores sold LeBron posters. If that was not enough LeBron presence for the true fan, it became possible to move James into your living room or bedroom in giant-sized fashion. Called a Fathead, the James (and other sports stars) human-sized stick-ons could be plastered to the wall almost like wallpaper.

The vivid James Fathead measured 38 inches wide by 79 inches tall and pictured him legs bent, leaping, cradling a basketball in his right hand, poised to dunk. The cut-off could be slapped on between items of furniture like bookcases, lamps, and chairs and the fan could have LeBron for company in his very own home. The price was $99, plus postage and handling; it was sold with the theme of "Get it. Peel it. Stick it. Five minutes and you're in the game."

James seemed to make as much news off the court as on it, but almost all things covered with a celebrity touch were light-hearted. Unlike some of his fellow high-profile athletes, James never made negative headlines because of run-ins with the law or security forces at nightclubs or by cracking up his car. James continued to be a good-news guy with his signature smile and his hardcore basketball work ethic. As the 2005–06 season wore on, it became apparent that the Cavaliers were fielding their best team in years and that a playoff run for success-starved fans was genuine.

On January 21, in a victory over the Utah Jazz, James fired in 51 points, collecting 32 of them in the second half. It seemed as if no time at all had passed, but James surpassed the 5,000-point mark for his career. Once again he was the youngest to reach the goal.

TOP ALL-STAR

In mid-season, James once again adjourned for the All-Star game. This was his second straight selection after being bypassed as a rookie to play in the Challenge game. Less than three weeks after learning of the vote, James emerged as the star of stars during the East's 122–120 win in Houston. James became the youngest player ever chosen as the Most Valuable Player following his 29-point, 6-rebound game. For that night he was on top of the world. Clouding the rest of the season and the Cavaliers' ability to make a run at a regular-season divisional title was surgery on a fractured Hughes finger that KO'd him from the lineup.

Some key games in March, as the regular season approached its end, signaled that the Cavaliers were ready to move to the hierarchy of the NBA and compete in the postseason. On March 19, Cleveland trailed the Los Angles Lakers by 18 points and rallied to win, 96–95. James was Cleveland's leading scorer with 29 points. Three days later, the Cavs came back to force overtime against Charlotte and defeat the Hornets, 120–118, with James exploding for 37 points. And a week later, Cleveland's 107–94 triumph over Dallas clinched the team's first playoff appearance since the 1997–98 season. At that moment it was easy to reflect on the tangible dividend of drafting LeBron James. The Cavs had become both a ticket-selling and critical success, as much as can be hoped for by any Broadway play. James scored 46 points and became the youngest player in league annals to pass 6,000 points. James was notching points 1,000 at a time, it seemed.

PLAYOFFS!

The playoff clincher was notable for several obvious reasons but also because the Cavaliers didn't take the race down to the final days of the season. They announced themselves as a postseason entry three weeks before the regular season's completion. The final regular-season record was

50–32, the team's first 50-win campaign since 1993. In the three seasons since James made his debut, the Cavaliers had engineered a 33-game turnaround. There was no doubt that James was the architect of the change. And again, James had improved his on-court performance. He averaged a startling 31.4 points per game, 7.0 rebounds, and 6.6 assists. Only all-time greats Oscar Robertson, Michael Jordan, and Jerry West had put together a trio of such impressive statistics in the three main measuring categories of performance. James played in 79 of the Cavaliers' 82 games and scored at least 20 points in 70 of them.

Qualifying for the playoffs was a goal that both James and the franchise had achieved. In the NBA they refer to the playoffs as the second season, however, and the Cavs desperately wanted to win a series. Cleveland matched up with the Washington Wizards in the first round of the Eastern Conference playoffs and the Cavs controlled the opener, 97–86, with James contributing a triple-double in all of his favorite box score categories.

The teams split the first four games, but the Cavaliers imposed their will in the two rugged wrap-up games, winning both in overtime to capture the club's first playoff series since 1993. James averaged 35.7 points a game for the six games and was in his own class during the series; performing far above the competition. But James and Cleveland needed help, and the supporting cast of Hughes (11.1 points), bouncing back from injury, forward Drew Gooden (8.2 points) and center Zydrunas Ilgauskus (10.4 points) ably aided the star.

The Cavaliers moved on with optimism and determination and played a hard-nosed series against the favored Detroit Pistons. Detroit, led by Chauncey Billups and Rasheed Wallace, looked like too high of a mountain to overcome. But just when analysts were proclaiming the Cavs finished, they roared back and won the next two games to knot the series. LeBron James, or not, however, the Pistons had too much depth for Cleveland and they closed out the Cavs in six games.

The season lasted about as long as Cleveland fans and players could have realistically wished, but the 50 wins and the postseason showing whetted James's appetite for more, and it proved that the Cavaliers would be a team to be reckoned with in the coming year. That is precisely what James thought after making the playoffs for the first time and cruising past the first round.

"It gave us a sense of confidence that we're one of the better teams in the league," he said. "But you know, on the other hand, we're one of the targeted teams. We can't sneak up on anybody, so that's a different feeling for us. We were able to sneak up on a few teams last year (2005–06) because we weren't as well known as we should have been. But now we're a better team and we have to uphold the standard that we have."[5]

After years of wandering aimlessly in the desert, the Cleveland Cavaliers' franchise had sipped greedily from a renewing reservoir of water—and a child had led them there.

THE LEAGUE TAKES NOTICE

In October 2006, LeBron James was back on the cover of *Sports Illustrated*. His featured appearance, along with other young NBA stars Carmelo Anthony and Dwayne Wade, represented something different than his cover appearance in high school. The first time, James was being announced to the world. This time, James, with his broad smile, distinctive headband above his forehead, and elaborate tattoos decorating his biceps, was truly being presented as King James, a leader of a young generation of stars carrying the NBA to new heights of popularity and accomplishment.

Having one's visage flashed on the cover of *Sports Illustrated* still symbolizes validation in the sports world that you are somebody special. But James had long before passed through such a stage of recognition. Before the 2005–06 season ended, he had been the subject of an extensive feature story in *GQ*. The *GQ* imprint made a statement about style and impact that goes beyond the basketball court. *GQ* readers are sometimes too grandly attired to get sweaty, so some of them were a new audience for LeBron examination. Splendidly attired in eye-catching suits on other occasions, James showed up for his *GQ* interview wearing a casual shirt that included the messages "Chosen 1" and "Gifted Child."

The interviewer concluded there was still a bit of mischievous little boy inside James, something James has never denied. For one thing, he was accompanied to the *GQ* interview by some of his homeboys, basketball playing teammates from St. Vincent-St. Mary. Some of those guys, Dru Joyce and Romeo Travis, among them, got the opportunity to stay home and play college ball for the University of Akron under old high school coach Keith Dambrot. When he got the chance during the basketball season, James dropped by to watch his old friends play.

James dined on pancakes, sausage, and bananas as he was quizzed, and once more, as in almost all in-depth looks from journalists, James came across as pretty much Superman on the court and preternaturally mature off of it. He did note "the special powers that I have been given." And he explained how his court vision—so widely praised—works. "Once I get comfortable with my surroundings out there, it seems like everything just slows down. I don't want to sound cocky when I say this, but it's like I see things before they happen. I kind of know where the defenders are gonna be. I kind of know where my teammates are gonna be, sometimes even before they know. My game is really played above time. I don't say that like I'm saying I'm ahead of my time. I'm saying, like, if I'm on the court and I throw a pass, the ball that I've thrown will lead a teammate right where he needs to go, before he even knows that that's the right place to go to. I just slow things down to a point where I can control what happens. It's a God-given talent."[6]

THE GIFTED LEBRON JAMES

The longer James played on the big stage, the more it became clear to basketball people that he spoke the truth when discussing God-given talent. Before James had completed his third season, Scottie Pippen, the Chicago Bulls forward voted one of the top 50 players in NBA history, and who was Michael Jordan's chief assistant in bringing six titles to the Windy City, saw James play. "He's growing into the greatest ever to play the game," Pippen said. For several years there had been routine pronouncements of players emerging as "the next Michael Jordan." Few dared whisper that there might be someone coming along so soon who might be better than Michael Jordan.[7]

One thing on the minds of fervent Cavaliers fans after James led the team to the playoffs at the end of the 2005–06 season was the fact that his rookie contract was finishing up and James could contemplate becoming a free agent. That was the worst nightmare scenario for Cleveland fans. The idea of watching James go off to a New York or Los Angeles and leading another team to a championship repelled them. James had that right. He just didn't have the inclination. He proved that his roots were as strong as ever in the Akron-Cleveland area by signing a three-year, $60 million deal locking him up with the Cavs through the 2009–10 season. The arrangement also called for a fourth-year player option, meaning James could stick around longer if he wanted. "Staying in Cleveland provides me with the unique opportunity to continue to play in front of my family, friends, and fans," James said.[8] Word of the contract leaked out about nine days before James inked it. The Cavaliers were so anxious to gain James's signature on the pact that the package was finalized not in Cleveland, but in Las Vegas, where James was practicing with the USA Basketball Men's Senior National Team, the squad competing in the World Championships in China.

The tournament site in Guangzhou served as a tune-up for China's scheduled hosting of the Beijing Summer Olympics in 2008, and the fans were rabid supporters of the home team when it faced the U.S. squad, even in a sport not nearly as popular as others in the world's largest country. The Americans were tested, but prevailed and James starred. "We just had to settle down," James said. "They were riding high off the fans. We wore them down in the second half. I don't look at myself as a hero. I just go out there and play my game and showcase my talent to the fans and take care of business."[9] Following its recent pattern of stumbling against other foreign teams, but playing just well enough to place, the U.S. team took home a bronze medal.

From the occasional rest, to making the occasional commercial, from representing his country on the basketball court, to working out for a fourth Cavaliers season, James had a varied and interesting summer after the 2006 playoffs ended. He found himself in situations that tested his playing ability and his poise, and he kept passing the tests. In a widely highlighted meeting, shortly before Cavaliers training camp opened in October for the 2006–07 season, James broke bread with investment king Warren Buffett, the Omaha, Nebraska business maven who is one of the richest men in the world. During a stop in Omaha, James rendezvoused with Buffett at the Crescent Moon Ale House to talk money. James, who gave Buffett one of his Cavalier jerseys, ate a hamburger and French fries and drank a milkshake. Buffett, who is regarded as one of the most astute assessors of stocks and financial markets in the world, counsels many wealthy investors. If anyone thought a tête-à-tête between James and Buffett was an odd-couple session, Buffett also previously met with New York Yankees third baseman Alex Rodriguez and with a businessman who bid $620,000 earmarked for charity to lunch with him.[10] If anyone was starry eyed walking away from the discussion, it seemed to be James, who characterized the meeting this way: "He's probably one of the best men I've ever met and it was the greatest experience I ever had. He's one of the most level-headed guys I know. It was a great experience."[11] James did not let listeners in on any stock tips.

Within days of meeting with Buffett, James made an appearance on "The Late Show with David Letterman." James shot hoops with Letterman outside the Ed Sullivan Theatre in New York City. And James also appeared on an MTV show called SportsBlender where he cracked jokes. The topic of the automobile the Chrysler LeBaron came up. No, it was not named for LeBron James.

During the prior season, Nike made hay with a clever group of commercials built around depicting James playing four separate roles on screen simultaneously. The shoe-buying public chuckled as James portrayed Wise LeBron, Business LeBron, Kid LeBron, and LeBron James the basketball guy. Nike brought the same foursome back a second time for the 2006–07 season and also authorized a four-pack set of James in all guises as collector statues. Michael Jordan symbolized the black athlete crossing over with endorsement appeal to the white fan. James was following in his footsteps the way no other black athlete was able to do. Michael Jordan's popularity seemed to transcend race. James seemed to have the same capability. People liked him regardless of the color of their own skins.

Right before the regular season began, James also acceded to a request to tape a segment of Comedy Central's "The Daily Show" with host Jon Stewart on The Ohio State University campus. In the parody news show, Stewart enthusiastically reviewed many of James's achievements and said, "I don't mean to be rude, but are you an alien creature?" Then Stewart asked James if even Kryptonite (Superman's weakness) could stop him. "At this point I'm not sure anything can stop me," James replied. Both the Letterman guest spot (which he had turned down four years earlier) and James's appearance on "The Daily Show" were signs he was more comfortable stepping out of the traditional role of a basketball player only. "I just got a little older," James said.[12]

Although he exhibited his playful moments with the television shows on his days off, James was primarily focused on basketball once the Cavaliers' preseason training camp opened on October 3. James, who before previous seasons set goals of a winning campaign and making it to the playoffs, was just as outspoken looking ahead. "We can win it all," he said. "We've just got to play well. Trying to win the whole thing is what's on my mind. There's no reason to play in the NBA if you don't think you can win it all."[13]

TIME TO WIN BIG

James admitted that going through the playoffs was an educational process that would only help the Cavaliers in their quest to go beyond the second round in the 2006–07 season, explaining how the intensity of the postseason is different from regular-season games in the middle of the winter. "Every possession counts," James said. "You can't take one possession off. You really feel it if you gamble, or you don't rotate on defense, or you miss a lay-up."[14]

As he began his fourth season in the NBA, James had grown into the stature of his reputation. First he merely wanted to try to prove himself on the court. Then he wanted to lift his team's status to contender. Too busy establishing himself among his peers and the public, James spent a few years deflecting praise heaped on him suggesting that he was to be the

NBA's savior. Before his fourth season, James all but announced he was ready to accept responsibility for becoming a major face of the league, if not the face of the league.

"Kids look up to us," James said. "They love the way we play the game of basketball, and they like some of the things we do off the court, so we are role models."[15]

For all of the respect shown to James by *Sports Illustrated* in its cover story, the magazine picked the Cavaliers as only the third best team in the Eastern Conference. Coach Mike Brown was depicted as looking through rose-colored glasses (a play on his ownership of 22 pairs of eyewear) when he said, "Last year was great, but our goal is to win the championship. We're going to try to get a little bit more movement, but make no mistake the ball is still going to be in LeBron's hands."[16]

Despite James's continuing improvement and Cleveland's mounting optimism, only the Cavaliers community foresaw a season where the Cavs might sweep to the NBA Finals.

NOTES

1. *Chicago Tribune*, June 26, 2005.

2. *Chicago Tribune*, November 14, 2005.

3. Sam Smith, *Chicago Tribune*, December 23, 2005.

4. *Chicago Tribune*, December 30, 2005.

5. LeBron James, press conference, Quicken Loans Arena, November 7, 2006.

6. Larry Platt, GQ *Magazine*, "The Fast Education of LeBron James," April, 2006.

7. Sam Smith, *Chicago Tribune*, May 19, 2006.

8. Associated Press, July 9, 2006.

9. USA Basketball Web Site game report, August 7, 2006.

10. Brian Windhorst, *Akron Beacon-Journal*, September 21, 2006.

11. Branson Wright, *Cleveland Plain Dealer*, October 3, 2006.

12. Julie Carr Smyth, Associated Press, November 1, 2006.

13. Wright, *Cleveland Plain Dealer*, October 3, 2006.

14. Wright, *Cleveland Plain Dealer*, October 3, 2006.

15. Chris Ballard, *Sports Illustrated*, October 23, 2006.

16. Marty Burns, *Sports Illustrated*, October 23, 2006.

Chapter 9

EARLY SEASON CHALLENGES

The action was hot at the Quicken Loans Arena—and the activity wasn't even on the court. Before the Cavaliers lined up for an early-season home game against the Atlanta Hawks, fans jammed the gift shop, competing for the right to buy souvenirs for the kids at home or the kids in the seats. It was possible to purchase a LeBron James anything, it seemed.

To dress like LeBron in a No. 23 Cavaliers jersey cost $80 (toddler size $60). A LeBron bobble-head doll sold for $28. Fans could buy a LeBron Christmas ornament for $15, an 8 by 10 color picture of LeBron for $6, an All-Star MVP pennant of LeBron for $8, or a mini-Cavs SUV LeBron car for $12. The team was doing its best to recoup some of its multimillion-dollar investment in James's contract. Whether it was attributable to James's personality and popularity, or a symbol of enlightenment in early twenty-first-century America, there were more white purchasers of James memorabilia than black buyers. Had James effectively rendered Cleveland colorblind?

The mood was buoyant. On November 4, four days earlier, in the second game of the 2006–07 season, the Cavaliers defeated one of the league's elite teams, the San Antonio Spurs, 88–81. It was the first time since 1988 that Cleveland bested San Antonio in Texas. James scored 35 points and said, "I was four years old the last time we beat San Antonio (there). I think for us to go out and be one of the powerhouses, which we've been preaching, we've got to go out there and walk the walk. We showed poise down the stretch. They made a run and we were able to withstand it."[1] When James first came into the league, any Cleveland-San Antonio game would have been summarized as a mismatch. To prove they belonged in faster company, the Cavaliers had to beat teams like San Antonio during the regular season. So even though the match-up occurred very early in the season it had psychic value for the Cavs.

On the night of the Hawks game, James was thoughtful during his meet-and-greet press conference outside the Cavaliers locker room. He had much on his mind about recent NBA developments. The NBA introduced a new basketball for the season, replacing the leather ball in use for decades with a ball made of synthetic material. The players, who were not consulted before the change, did not like the new ball. Most called it slippery. James, who had experience with the new ball when it was experimental in the prior year's All-Star game, had been successful with it, but disliked the feel.

"With the leather ball you know what you're going to get every game," James said. "But the new ball, sometimes dribbling during the game, it sticks to your hand. It doesn't get as much bounce if you want to throw a bounce pass. It will just roll on you, and it won't bounce up in the air like the old ball. Sometimes it's good and sometimes it's not."[2] It was a significant change for players whose livelihood depended on ball handling, on being able to make sure passes, to control the ball on fancy dribbles, and they were aghast when confronted by a poor grip when they rose for a jump shot. The backlash, from stars like James, as well as other players, grew so loud that midway through the season Commissioner David Stern backtracked, removed the new balls, and replaced them with the tried-and-true standby leather balls.

A new rule for the season also seemed to give referees extra power to crack down on demonstrative players. The league goal was to control the number of technical fouls, prevent physical showboating, and players' sassy responses to calls that seemed to flaunt officials' authority. But there had already been cases of overzealous whistling that put some players on edge. An emotional player like James, who wanted to pump up his team, worried that he could get slammed with a technical foul providing the other team with a free foul shot and possession of the ball just by being true to his feelings. "I've always been passionate about the game, but I have to be cool," James said, concerned that even a minimalist Peyton Manning hands-raised, touchdown pass celebration would be deemed offensive. Whether or not there was a directive from the league urging refs to cool their jets, after the initial break-in period, the calls seemed to mellow out and the threat of being whistled for technical fouls did not bother James the rest of the season.[3]

NEW HABITS

James revealed a secret—he had awakened barely an hour earlier. On the day the Cavs faced the Hawks James had snoozed for hours. He was practically rubbing the sleep out of his eyes when he reached The Q a little bit after 5 p.m. He had a pre-game routine in place. After the morning shoot-around focused on that night's opponent, James developed the habit of going home or to the team hotel for some shut-eye. "I am a nap guy," James said with a laugh. "I try to get four hours of rest before the game and then I'm pretty well ready. If anything is going on between 12 and 4 p.m. I'll probably miss it."[4]

Starting his fourth year in the NBA, James's stature as one of the most prominent players had been established. He had shown that he could make Cleveland a winner. James had impressively shown that his high school fanfare was not fraudulent. NBA veterans tend to be jaded when they read in magazines or see on television about the latest phenom. They have a show-me attitude because there is always a freshly hyped player coming along who it is said will be one of the all-time greats. They disdain such coverage and try not to be swayed by it. When the real deal does show up, however, they recognize it. James had passed beyond the range of skepticism.

"Until some guy comes along and proves it, it's sort of 'OK, I'll believe it when I see it,'" said Cavalier guard Eric Snow. "But playing with the best guys, you've got a chance to win, to be out there and have a chance to win every night."[5]

James seemed aware that Snow was prone to make such diplomatic statements. After James appeared on "The Daily Show" near mid-term Congressional elections, he told Cleveland reporters he had no political ambitions, but when they pressed him for an opinion on which teammate would make the best politician, James replied, "E. Snow."[6] It was also possible that James picked the wrong political teammate. Guard Larry Hughes was asked what his campaign slogan would be if he ever ran for governor in his home state of Missouri and he said, "Free money for everyone. That would definitely get me elected."[7]

Different players bring different perspectives to a team and to the outlook of teaming up with a star who commands so much attention. Shannon Brown, a rookie out of Michigan State, had just joined the Cavaliers. Even though he knew all about James, he had not known him well and Brown had not experienced the rock-star, circus-like atmosphere that follows James everywhere on the basketball circuit.

"I was fortunate enough to come to a great team on the rise," said Brown, the Cavaliers' 2006 first-round draft pick. "It's really unexplainable how much he brings to this town. He brings a lot of excitement, as far as what he does on the court, and how he carries himself. He's just a cool, down-to-earth guy to be around, a great person."[8]

THE JAMES EFFECT ON CLEVELAND

Mike Brown was starting his second season as Cavaliers coach. He was part of the new management team that took over the club after owner Gordon Gund sold out to Dan Gilbert. Paul Silas got James in his growing-pains years. Brown was supposed to reap the benefits of James's sophistication. He had already guided the Cavaliers to their breakthrough play-off appearance, with James averaging more than 30 points a game. Now more was expected from both of them. Brown was the management bridge to the star player. He was in closer contact, more often, with him than anyone else connected to the front office. As coach, Brown was also the man who had to be the most attuned to James's circumstances, conditioning, and health. Most of the time Brown deals with Xs and Os, but even he could not stop marveling at the outsized impact LeBron James made on his hometown team and his hometown area.

"It's economically off the charts," Brown said. "Not just Cleveland, but Cleveland and the surrounding areas, I'd even say the whole state of Ohio. He's a fantastic draw to have and a homegrown product. I can't even explain what he's done to the area. He's also given the people a sort of hope, or belief, or the confidence to walk around with their chests puffed out knowing that LeBron James is from here and he plays here. It's a great feeling to have." Brown said it is remarkable how many kids, adults, grandparents, and fans walk around Cleveland wearing LeBron James jerseys and offered a $100 reward if an observer could count the number of spectators among the 20,000 fans in the building that night wearing them.[9] It proved impossible to make an accurate count, but neither age nor skin color made a difference in the wearers. Cavs fans were united by their James jerseys.

The Atlanta Hawks were a bad team at the beginning of the 2005–06 season, one of the teams that had replaced the Cavaliers of a few years earlier in the basement of the NBA. The Hawks figured to be easy prey for the Cavs early in the season, with a throng of fans screaming, fireworks going off in the arena, and flattering videos introducing the players flashing on the scoreboard. The building was rocking and rolling and about as loud as it would be for a rock and roll concert. Yet the Cavaliers had trouble with the focused Hawks right from the opening tip. It was 20–20 after one quarter, a low-scoring 38–37 Cavs at the half, and 90–90 at the end of regulation play. Cleveland was sent into overtime by the lowly Hawks and lost, 104–95.

James was his usual lead-the-way self, with 34 points, 7 rebounds and 6 assists, but Hawks guard Joe Johnson's 25 points and an unanticipated 19 points and 11 assists from Atlanta guard Tyronn Lue offset James's showing. James also hit only 5 of 11 free throws, costly mistakes. The game was indicative of many things in the NBA. To be a truly dominant team with first-place aspirations, the Cavaliers had to brush aside challenges from clubs like the Hawks. It also showed that it is a long season and that truly on any given night a weaker team might play better and upend a more balanced squad. And it demonstrated that even a lightly regarded team can count on heady veterans like Johnson and Lue at various points in the season. The Hawks outplayed the Cavaliers in the fourth quarter and overtime when it mattered most. Yes, the Cavaliers had LeBron James, the best player on the court, and possibly the best player in the league, but he could not single handedly lead his team to wins every night. These were all lessons to be remembered and stored for later in the season when the Cavs hoped to be operating on all cylinders and motoring to the playoffs.

James was reflective in the locker room. Basketball, baseball, and hockey players play so many games so bunched together that redemption is just around the corner. They have time to study game films to make adjustments, but they do not have time to brood over losses and fixate on what happened in the recent past. They must move on quickly and make sure they do not get stuck in ruts that cause repeat mistakes. They must absorb the education from a beating overnight and translate it into an adjustment before the next team comes along.

"They shot the ball extremely well from the three-point line," James said. "I thought we got their attention with some tough shots, but Tyronn has hurt us in the past and he hurt us tonight. It will be interesting to go back and watch the tape. I think we probably relaxed a little bit and they turned it up a notch. I've said many times you've got to play for 48 minutes. We didn't and they got back in the game and that gave them the confidence and opportunity to win down the stretch."[10]

After he issued his analysis, James sat at his locker for a bit, naked from the waist up, his powerful upper body muscles rippling, wearing just a towel. In high school at St. Vincent-St. Mary, a single loss seemed like a disaster and was almost enough to bring the Fighting Irish to tears. In the pros, the losses accumulated during the regular-season get filed away quickly. The Cavaliers' next game chance was only two days away.

If the fans were left sighing instead of applauding, the trip downtown was worthwhile for them anyway. The heavily advertised promotion of the game was the season's LeBron James Bobble-Head night. Thousands of fans retreated into the night clutching their precious gift, even if they couldn't smile about a victory.

CAN NICE GUYS FINISH FIRST?

Roy Campanella, the Hall of Fame catcher for the Brooklyn Dodgers, once said that to be a Major League Baseball star you had to have some little boy in you. LeBron James personified that in basketball. He was at the top of the world in basketball, but at 21 he still was frisky and playful and enjoyed mingling with kids and young people. That was one reason why he expanded his appearances to light-hearted television programs like "The Daily Show" and "The Late Show with David Letterman."

"You've got to have fun with it," James said of his basketball fame. "You don't ever want to get to the point where it's like just business. I don't go into those things to raise my profile, or raise my status. I just go on there because I like to do those things and it's kind of fun for me. They were both fun."[11]

James schedules many activities that bring him into contact with youngsters in his home town of Akron, and said he hopes his achievements bring more attention to the quality of the city's hoops. He supervised a basketball camp and said maybe some of the campers would grow up to be college players or pros. "It's hopefully very important to the kids to have the opportunity to play basketball," he said. "Hopefully we can inspire some good kids to get out there who want to play."[12]

It has been established in the public mind that James is a young man who likes to enjoy himself in rather tame ways—not getting into after-hours troubles—and his smile is as much of a trademark as his jump shot. Except when he is playing serious basketball, on the court for the Cavaliers, it is hard to find photographs of him where he is not smiling. A magazine story at the start of James's fourth year of play was headlined, "Don't Let The Smile Fool You." In the article, Cavaliers assistant general manager Lance Blanks described James as "the consummate extrovert. LeBron doesn't have a self-conscious bone in his body. Throw on Jim Jones's 'We Fly High' and see him start grooving.'" The story's writer called James "the anti-loner." James admitted it and said that's one reason he spends so much time with his old buds from Akron and St. Vincent-St. Mary. "I'm an outgoing person," James said. "I like to share the comedy and what I do every day. I'd go crazy if I was by myself."[13]

Sometimes famous athletes who surround themselves with an entourage are ridiculed for traveling with a posse. Sometimes, as they say, in a world that treats them as an idol, rushes them for autographs, and surrounds them when they step outside, it is a way of "keeping it real." James naturally wants to share his good fortune with his old friends, according to Romeo Travis, one of those former St. Vincent-St. Mary teammates who played at the University of Akron. "He wants to be the main course, but he wants everybody on the plate with him," Travis said.[14]

Part of the context for the magazine article was whether or not James could remain a nice guy and become one of the NBA's greatest players. He did not, it was established by observers and James himself, have the same intense killer instinct as Michael Jordan or the Lakers' Kobe Bryant. But what James was proving in his fourth season as the Cavaliers played like more of a veteran team was that his superstar abilities could carry his team to victories without displaying such a hardcore attitude.

BREAKING OTHER TEAMS

Shortly after the Cavaliers' disappointing loss to the Atlanta Hawks, they faced the Chicago Bulls at Quicken Loans Arena. In some ways this was an important game because the team wanted to put the bad taste of the Hawks loss in the rearview mirror and because the Bulls are in the same division. Head-to-head play could become a tiebreaker in the final standings or make a difference in home-court advantage during the playoffs.

Except for Wilt Chamberlain in the distant past and Shaquille O'Neal in the current NBA, superstars are counted on to make their free throws, especially at crunch time in close games. James fretted over his 5-of-11 day versus Atlanta before the Bulls game. "It's just going up there and making them," he said of the natural way of shooting that blanks out thinking. "You know when you're making them. It feels good. When you miss, it doesn't feel too good, so you just have to get back on focusing on free throws. I think with free throws it can become mental at times. Any guy knows you can go through one of those cold streaks at the line and it can become mental. Every time you go up there, and you're by yourself, people think it's a freebie, but it's probably one of the most difficult shots in the game."[15]

James was hinting that he hadn't really gotten over his sub-par free-throw shooting against Atlanta. The Bulls were not counting on it happening again, though. Their pre-game workouts and chalk talk concentrated on the best ways to contain James. They knew they had to beat James if they were going to beat the Cavaliers. But veteran players also know that James's ascension to one of the league's top players is good for all of them in terms of hype, attention, and fan enthusiasm.

"There's no doubt," said forward P. J. Brown, who has played with the Bulls, New Jersey Nets, Miami Heat, and the Charlotte Hornets. "He's a guy who draws like a magnet. He draws your attention, no matter what, whether you're an avid basketball fan, or somebody who just happens to see him. You hear his name and he's one of those types of guys where you've got to stop and see what he's doing because you never know what he's going to do on a night-to-night basis.

"Sometimes they crown guys too fast, too early. We bestow the honor on them before they even earn it, you know, 'the next Jordan, (Larry) Bird, Magic (Johnson).' They received all of the recognition, the glory, but it was a process. They earned it. I just think it's unfair to guys who've been in the league for a long time, who put a lot of time in. LeBron, I think he's exceeded expectations. There's no doubt about it. He's a great player. He's shown it, but he still has to take his team to the ultimate level."[16]

Before the Bulls showdown, Chicago coach Scott Skiles contemplated ways to slow down James and take him out of position to dominate, so the Bulls could have a happy ending. Skiles made it sound as if there was almost no way for the Bulls to prevent James from going off with a good game no matter what type of defense they threw at him or which forwards. "Well, we have more bodies (than the year before)," Skiles said, "but just because you're throwing a body out there doesn't mean anything other than it's a body, you know. I mean he can pretty much get what he wants to with the ball. For instance, one of those guys tonight will be in their fifth NBA game guarding one of the best in the world. Ultimately, it's a tall order in their first game against him."

Luol Deng, the Bulls' second-year forward, had already seen his share of James on the court the year before as a rookie, and he had nothing but praise for the slippery-to-cover star. "His game is so complete," Deng said. "He'll post up, or bring it off the dribble. We have to challenge every shot he takes and make him uncomfortable."[17] The thought was accurate, but it failed to consider that James is nowhere more comfortable in the world than when he has the ball in his hands on the basketball court.

Atlanta Coach Mike Woodson had suggested that James was going to be one of the best players of all time, but Skiles jokingly asked if Woodson said it before the game or after defeating the Cavs. It was after. "He was in a good mood," Skiles said. "I think he's (James) obviously a great, great player in today's game. It's hard to compare guys from before. And you know, I think before we start saying that about people they should have a title under their belt. They should have things under their belt that just makes that a logical conclusion."[18]

A STATEMENT GAME

The Cavaliers and James looked like championship material less than an hour later when they burst to a 30–18 lead over the Bulls. Only rarely during the course of the game did Chicago make a run that made it seem possible the Bulls would catch up. It was a Cleveland night all the way. The Cavs won 98–79 and James contributed 19 points and 12 assists. Free throws were not an issue. The flaw seemed cured when James made seven of eight tries.

It was clear that the Bulls had no answer for James. But neither did any other team in the league. "I think he's one of the fastest guys and he's maybe 260 pounds, in that neighborhood," Skiles said, "and the way he can run up and down the floor . . . and his jumping is underrated. He can fly from end-to-end."[19]

For one of the rare times during the season, the Cavaliers' top scorer was not James, but forward Drew Gooden, who scored 20 points. Gooden's mixed bag of mid-range jumpers and inside power moves killed the Bulls. Gooden said the Cavaliers learned quickly from their lackadaisical loss to the Hawks, pinning that defeat on overconfidence left over from the previous season's playoff run. "We thought we could approach games like we were already frontrunners in the NBA, and we can't do that," Gooden said.[20]

The Cavs hit 57 percent of their shots from the field, something that bothered the defensively minded Bulls considerably. "They pretty much had their way with us," lamented Skiles.[21]

The Cavaliers sent 19,947 fans home happy and captured their fifth straight decision from the Bulls. It was a message to Chicago that it might be better off spending the winter hoping for a less difficult playoff match-up.

NOTES

1. Associated Press, November 4, 2006.

2. LeBron James, press conference, Quicken Loans Arena, November 7, 2006.

3. James, press conference.

4. James, press conference.

5. Eric Snow, press conference, Quicken Loans Arena, November 7, 2006.

6. Mary Schmitt Boyer, *Cleveland Plain Dealer*, November 6, 2007.

7. Branson Wright, *Cleveland Plain Dealer*, November 8, 2006.

8. Shannon Brown, press conference, Quicken Loans Arena, November 7, 2006.

9. Mike Brown, press conference, Quicken Loans Arena, November 7, 2006.

10. James, press conference, November 7, 2006.

11. LeBron James, press conference, Quicken Loans Arena, November 9, 2006.

12. James, press conference, November 9, 2006.

13. Chris Broussard, *ESPN The Magazine*, "Don't Let The Smile Fool You," November 6, 2006.

14. Broussard, *ESPN The Magazine*.

15. James, press conference, November 9, 2006.

16. P.J. Brown, press conference, Quicken Loans Arena, November 9, 2006.

17. K.C. Johnson, *Chicago Tribune*, November 9, 2006.

18. Scott Skiles, press conference, Quicken Loans Arena, November 9, 2006.

19. Skiles, press conference, November 9, 2006.

20. Branson Wright, *Cleveland Plain Dealer*, November 10, 2006.

21. John Jackson, *Chicago Sun-Times*, November 10, 2006.

Chapter 10

ON A CHRISTMAS ROLL

The early-season concerns were obliterated quickly. LeBron James and the Cavaliers played with more confidence than ever at the start of the 2006–07 NBA season. There *was* a carryover—a healthy one—from the preceding playoff season.

Even when the Cavaliers stumbled out of the starting gate, that no longer meant they were doomed in a game. In mid-November, the Boston Celtics built a 19-point lead over Cleveland, only to see the Cavs storm back for a 94–93 triumph. James scored 38 points, 25 of them in the second half when the Cavaliers rallied. There was no give up in the Cavaliers, where not too many years ago trailing 25–6 might have meant the result could be mailed in. Those were the old Cavs, not the new Cavs. "We could have easily packed it in, but that's not who I am," James said. "Any time I'm on the court, it doesn't matter how many points we're down, we always have a chance to win."[1]

Guard Larry Hughes had suffered a fresh injury and was forced to sit out in early December, and on the night he returned to the lineup, key forward Drew Gooden went down. But neither getting used to the return of Hughes, nor the loss of Gooden slowed the Cavaliers. They crushed the Indiana Pacers, 107–75. The 32-point blowout was symbolic of how far the team had come since its disappointing loss to the Atlanta Hawks in November. The Cavaliers were beginning to flex muscles they didn't even know they had and were making sure they beat the teams they were supposed to beat. Their record of 12–7 was good, not spectacular, but things were jelling. James totaled a game-high 27 points, but he scored

24 points in the first half to propel Cleveland to its insurmountable lead before resting much of the second half. "We did a good job of jumping on a team and not letting up," said a satisfied James.[2] A glance at the stat sheet confirmed James's comment. Cleveland shot 68.4 percent from the floor in the first half, a phenomenal rate, and led by 15 points at the end of the first 12 minutes.

Although the Cavaliers' sizzling shooting cooled off in the second half as more backups got playing time, one of the signals of how Cleveland could dominate was with ball movement. Defenses always tended to focus on James. Sometimes he took it right to them and scored, as he did in the first half. Other times he was pleased to pass off to open teammates. He had displayed the same discipline and keen judgment since he was in high school playing with Dru Joyce, Romeo Travis, and the rest of the Fighting Irish. James contributed six assists, but when a leader involves all of the other players and is willing to pass first, instead of shoot, it can be contagious. When a whole team takes that approach it can prove devastating. "We've always been able to share the ball," James said. "We made extra passes and guys were able to finish. We wanted to try to execute as much as possible, and we were able to do that."[3]

It didn't take long for the NBA to digest its star players' disdain for the new synthetic ball. The Players Association actually filed an unfair labor practices charge. James, who was as vociferous as anyone in protesting about the implementation of the new ball when the season began in early November, like other players was glad for the reprieve when Commissioner David Stern backtracked with an announcement December 11 that the ball was being shelved for further study.

"That's how we make our living," Chicago Bulls forward P. J. Brown said of coping with the hard-to-handle ball. "The game revolves around that ball. I think people took it too lightly and took it upon themselves to change it. I think you definitely have to get input from the main guys (around the league)—(Steve) Nash, (a two-time MVP), (Jason) Kidd (New Jersey's star ball handler), LeBron, Shaq (four-time champion Shaquille O'Neal)."[4]

James was content that the switch was made. "I'm a very big supporter of the leather ball, so I'm very happy about the change," he said.[5]

BASKETBALL IS A SMALL WORLD AFTER ALL

In the early days of the NBA, rivalries were fierce between teams and players. During the 1950s, when there were only eight teams, it seemed to players and fans that they played one another every other day. In an era when games were called more loosely, more elbows were thrown and contact was rougher. It was rare to be pals with regulars on the other team. The evolution of basketball in the United States brought about different attitudes, probably by the 1980s, definitely by the 1990s, and quite markedly by the 2000s. Players on different teams in the NBA did not often play against one another if they were divided between the Eastern Conference and the Western Conference. Ordinarily, that would indicate they hardly knew one another. With the proliferation of summer traveling teams such as the Amateur Athletic Union (AAU) crew LeBron James played with, however, summer all-star games dotted around the country, and with college teams playing more national schedules, a player who grew up in West Virginia might now become close to a player who grew up in Oregon.

The Cavaliers and the Chicago Bulls are divisional rivals. Success by one of those teams might come at the expense of the other. Yet LeBron James, African American star forward for Cleveland, and Kirk Hinrich, white star guard for Chicago by way of Kansas University, developed a friendship. They found common ground sharing time together on the 2006 U.S. World Championship team. The topic arose each time the NBA teams met in November and December.

"I think we've become good friends," James said of the hard-nosed, scrappy player. "Especially, you know, being together for 35 or 36 days. He is a good friend of mine. I respect the way he handles himself, the way he respects the game of basketball and the way he approaches it."[6]

The Cavaliers manhandled the Bulls that night in Cleveland. The next time the teams met was in Chicago, at the United Center, on December 30, James's birthday. Once again it was asked, What do you get the millionaire who has everything? James said he did not have a long list of needs or wants. "Just a win," he said, which is what most people who knew him expected he would say. Then James returned to the subject of playing against his new close friend Hinrich. "I love Kirk's game. I love him as a person. You know when you see him on the court or off the court that he loves the game of basketball. He doesn't take any possessions off. I think they've got one great player in Chicago."[7]

Hinrich said that he and James hit it off particularly well when Team USA was in China for the world championships. Being a small group of Americans in Asia at a time when security is heavy for those wearing red, white, and blue and representing the United States meant that it was difficult to wander around and blend. Usually, he said, the players stuck together. Hinrich said he hardly knew James before the team went overseas.

"Just a little bit, from being in the same practices," Hinrich said. "But you know, it was a long summer where the whole team was together. I got to know him and like him."

James has been known to let loose by dancing, but Hinrich, who keeps his sashaying to a minimum, burst out laughing when it was suggested they might have boogied together. "No," he said. "But we were in a different country so all of the guys kind of hung out together. He's a good guy. We became friends. What makes him an elite player is his size and knowledge of the game. He's 6-foot-8 and he passes so well. The tough thing about him is his athleticism and he's hard to match up with. You've either got a guy on him that's smaller or a guy that's too big. He's probably one of the fastest guys in the league. When he gets going, with a head of steam, he's hard to stop. I think when you first see it, you're like, 'Wow!' because he just flies up and down the court. Seriously, he's one of the fastest guys in the league."[8]

With the year poised to turn to 2007, the divisional match-up between Cleveland and Chicago once again loomed as (in the vernacular) "a statement game," but also as one that had a tangible effect on the standings. The Cavaliers thumped Chicago in Cleveland in November and the Bulls were spoiling for another fight. They had righted themselves and at the time of the game, the Bulls boasted an 18–12 record to Cleveland's 17–11. A Cavaliers victory would move them ahead of Chicago.

Even with a meaningful regular-season game on tap, the mood was light in the hours leading up to tip-off. There was the pleasant James and Hinrich mutual admiration society discussion and some light-hearted talk about James's birthday. James denied having any special plans away from the court in Chicago and emphasized his single-minded stance about a present. "Trying to get a win for my birthday," James reiterated. "That would be the best thing that would happen for me." To obtain that victory, though, James realized the Cavaliers would have to outsmart the Bulls again and that it might not be as easy to do so as it was in Cleveland about seven weeks earlier. "I've seen every defense an NBA team can put on me," he said, "and on our team. So you know we have to adjust to whatever defensive strategy goes on in the course of the game."

PROVING POINTS

James was aware that there were still some Cavaliers skeptics who didn't believe that the previous season's playoff run meant much and that even the six games above .500 record was less worthy than it read, because many wins were over weak teams. He was unfazed. "We don't judge ourselves by what everybody else is saying," James said. "We're second in our division and I think second or third in the whole Eastern Conference. We're playing really good basketball right now."[9]

Cavs Coach Mike Brown said he had no secret birthday presents prepared to hand over to his star in the locker room. No Teddy bears or such surprises and when he was informed James said all he wanted was a win, Brown said, "Me, too."[10]

When the game began, the Bulls were carrying the burden of five straight losses to the Cavaliers. This time they were at home, though, and did everything right to excite the 22,965 spectators in the United Center. Forward Luol Deng bombed away for 32 points and sharp-shooting guard Ben Gordon flipped in 21 points. James countered with 33 points, but the overdue Bulls had the upper hand, winning 103–96. A stunning stretch at the end of the third quarter, overlapping into the fourth quarter, decided the game. The Bulls went on a 24–0 run. The Cavs missed 14 straight shots from the field and did not score a point for 9 minutes and 50 seconds. James did not get the birthday present he coveted.

"They went on that big run and that killed us," James said. "They moved the ball and picked it up defensively."[11]

Deng put up the biggest numbers for the Bulls, but as he had proven during his short time in the league, Gordon was instant offense off the bench. Coach Scott Skiles used the former University of Connecticut All-American to give his team a boost when the starters tired. Many times Gordon had erupted with his near-unstoppable jump shot to slay foes. During a pre-game scouting report of sorts, James had issued a warning that the Cavaliers must watch out for Gordon. "He's coming off the bench, but he gets a lot of intensity going," James said. "He has the green light. He is a very great scorer and he can be a starter on all 30 teams in this league, of course."[12] Prescient, James was right about the Bulls' secret weapon's performance that night.

The loudest noise in the Cavaliers' locker room after the loss was the hissing sound of showers. There was no fooling around after a defeat, no blasting music being played. But professional athletes do not let a hard-fought, regular-season defeat bring them too far down emotionally, either. James did not get what he wished for on the day he turned 22 years old, but he wasn't going to complain too loudly, either. "Chicago's a great, great team at home. As well as we are," James said. "We are 1-1 in the series. I'm not letting it spoil my birthday."[13]

It was a reminder that the NBA season is very long and that many games remained before the regular season ended in April.

FITNESS KING

On the first Sunday of the new year in January 2007, Americans awoke to the sight of King James telling them to do pushups and sit-ups and to run around the block so they could be healthier and improve their fitness. Be like LeBron. James and his broad smile were pictured on the front cover of *Parade* magazine, the Sunday supplement that appears in millions of copies of newspapers each week. The command on the front cover was: "Get Fit Now!" Clearly, the timing was linked to Americans' mania for New Year's resolutions to lose weight.

Inside the magazine, the article was illustrated with a picture of James competing in a joke-like tug-of-war with Olympic volleyball gold medalists Kerri Walsh and Misty May-Treanor. The athletes were used primarily as attention-getters and advice from a panel of doctors was the main thrust of the story; however, James got his say. "A good workout can be relaxing—and we all need to break a sweat every now and then," he said.[14] The use of James's visage on the cover of *Parade* was another way to break through to a mainstream American audience from someone perceived as "just" a star basketball player.

LeBron James the marketing genius was off to a fast start in 2007, but so was LeBron James the Cleveland Cavaliers' basketball player. On January 3, the Cavs bested the Boston Celtics, 107–104. Earlier in the season, it took a rally from 19 points down for Cleveland to surpass Boston. This time it was a war all the way. The man who delivered the game-deciding shots was "Mr. Clutch," James. Near game's end in Boston's TD Banknorth Garden, James tossed in a devastating jump shot off the backboard from near the visitor's bench and then he iced the contest by hitting two free throws.

"A lot of people say I can't shoot free throws, but at the end of the day I want the ball," James said of his critics. "If I make them, it's good. If I miss them I got to take responsibility. But at the end of the ballgame, when we need to make two free throws, I want the ball."[15]

Being viewed as an everyday star in the NBA is one way to obtain status. Being viewed as a go-to player whose team can count on a player in crunch time is another thing altogether. Until a player converts a number of opportunities to come through, he cannot obtain the second layer of status. James was on his way. Even earlier in the game, he displayed some run-out-the-clock-defying moments. James sank a bucket with just

.2 seconds left on the clock before halftime. He made a buzzer beater at the end of the third quarter, and he scored the last points of the game with 7.6 seconds remaining.

The most spectacular play occurred at the end of the third quarter. Early in his Cleveland career, James filmed a Powerade commercial where he repeatedly hit jump shots that floated most of the length of the court. In this real-life game situation, he got the ball just beyond the end line 94 feet from the hoop and heaved an 83-foot shot that bounced off the backboard and through the basket. "After I launched it," James said, "I heard the game clock go off, so I knew it was good. The way I shot it, I knew I had a chance. I practice that. Every day after practice me and Drew (teammate Drew Gooden) shoot trick shots like that and (it) was one of those days that I got one off and it went in."[16]

Such rare long-range shots—worth three points—create considerable buzz in an arena, but don't count for more than a regular 22-foot-plus shot. James noted that making his two free throws were bigger plays at the time, if not as flashy, because, with time running out, the Celtics were forced to attempt a three-point shot merely to tie. "The two free throws were big," he said. "They made the Celtics come down and shoot a contested jump shot or a contested three. So the free throws were bigger than the long three."[17]

James finished the game with 32 points, but also the biggest points scored at the most pressurized times. By his fourth season, it was a given that James was the take-charge player on the Cavaliers' roster. He expected to have choices with the ball in key situations, not to have to beg for the ball. The team, with the backing of Coach Mike Brown, recognized it, too. "He's our man and I have faith in him," Brown said after James' Boston performance. "I want the ball in his hands any given night and I have faith we will win more than we will lose with him."[18]

AMERICA FINDS OUT ABOUT LEBRON

The selling of the LeBron James name and imprinting it in the public marketplace continued at full speed. Coca-Cola, one of James's early sponsors, embarked on a new campaign to bond James with Sprite. The company announced a contest seeking a theme song linking the basketball player and the soft drink. Fans were able to submit entries and then vote on their favorite tunes through a Web site. The Supreme Court justice in the competition—chief judge—was James, who called it "an honor" to be the subject of a theme song created specifically for him.[19]

An intriguing and rather rare moment arrived on the court for James in an early January game against the Milwaukee Bucks—James failed to score in double figures, yet his team won anyway. It was an unpremeditated answer to basketball skeptics who still considered the Cavaliers a one-man team that would go nowhere without James being at the top of his game. The 95–86 victory was proof that Cleveland could win on a LeBron off-day. James attempted only 13 shots, made just three, and scored just eight points, although he added nine assists. Drew Gooden scored 31 points with 16 rebounds to make up for James's lack of production. "I mean, 13 shots for me, and a win," James said. "Eight points, but we got a win. Any time my teammates pick it up for me like that it's great to see." Mike Brown said he was pleased that James persevered on a night when his shot was off and he concentrated on defense and passing to help the team. "I'm proud of LeBron James because they jumped him the whole night and he struggled a bit offensively," Brown said.[20]

James had established himself as an NBA phenomenon the season before when he earned the Most Valuable Player award in the all-star game. It was clear then that James was likely to become a many-time all-star in the years to come. What he didn't expect at the end of January was the final vote totals for the 2006–07 team for the February game in Las Vegas. James received more than 2.5 million votes to lead all players. The vote made him a three-time selection, but James seemed genuinely shocked that he led vote-getters at all positions. "That's something I've never dreamed of," he said. "I've always wanted to be an all-star, but being the leading vote-getter over guys like Vince Carter, Shaquille O'Neal, Dwayne Wade, and Allen Iverson, you never think that's going to happen. Just getting the opportunity to be the leading vote-getter is kind of unbelievable."[21]

The Cavaliers showed they could win on a LeBron bad day, but at the end of January they also got to show they could win a game without LeBron altogether. James was sidelined by a sprained right toe injured in a game against Denver on January 19 that had passed MRI inspection, but that was rested for a January 26 contest against the Philadelphia 76ers. The Cavs won anyway, 105–97, in Philadelphia. "If it was a playoff game he could play," Mike Brown said. "The doctor suggested it would be good to give him the additional rest. It's just sore."[22] The Cavaliers wanted James's toe where no one could step on it while jumping up and down in rebounding action and the bench seemed as safe a place as any.

James's passion for playing superseded his toe trouble and he returned to the Cleveland lineup one game later, only to lose 115–100 to the Phoenix Suns. Whether James re-sprained the toe or just jammed it, he said he was going to miss more playing time and would take it easy to avoid long-term injury. "It's definitely going to take time for me," James said. "I really have to get off of it. It's definitely a problem. I can't keep forcing action."[23]

James was healthy before the All-Star game rolled around in mid-February. It was a time when many basketball reporters took stock of James and his impact on the league and a time when James's playful side was on display. Cleveland sports columnist Bill Livingston analyzed the various sides of James's personality in relation to the four-LeBron Nike commercial, noting that just when fans think they know James he shows them something new.

Livingston not only talked to people who know James well, he asked James about the four LeBrons in the commercial and speculated that James may still be running behind Indianapolis Colts quarterback Peyton Manning as the all-sport "mega-endorser leader." Not that James would admit it. "But asked whose commercials are better," Livingston wrote, "James playfully said: 'Mine, of course. I play four roles and he only plays one. He's only working three hours. I was working 12.'"[24]

STILL A STAR

The NBA All-Star break is not only about a mid-season rest for teams playing a long schedule stretching from November to April before the playoffs. It is showtime and a time to show off for the sport's biggest names. Players display their three-point shooting skills and their flashiest slam dunk skills, mingle with the fans, and make friends for the league. James is a natural in that environment. When he got news that he was the top vote-getter, James said, "It's always special to be a part of All-Star weekend. I think the No. 1 reason is because the fans vote you in. It's the one opportunity in the NBA season where the fans can bring all the best players to one venue. It makes it a little bit more special that it's in Las Vegas. It's a city that a lot of people love. It's about the stars in Vegas and then you're bringing all the NBA stars there."[25]

No big deal was made of it at the time, but there was an irony in James participating in an NBA neutral-court All-Star game in Las Vegas. Those with long memories recalled that when he was drafted he predicted his basketball skills would light up Cleveland like Las Vegas. In this instance—with that mission accomplished—James was exporting his Cleveland basketball skills to help light up Vegas.

James did not win a second consecutive All-Star game MVP award. That honor went to the Lakers' Kobe Bryant with his 31 points in the Western Conference's 153–132 triumph over the East. But James was the top gun in the Eastern Conference with 28 points, 6 rebounds, and 6 assists. Even though it was an exhibition game, James was disappointed by the loss. He lamented the West's fast start and consistency that stalled any East comebacks.

The All-Star game is a diversion. The second half of the regular season is when teams in contention for the playoffs jockey for position. They fight it out to win division titles and to claim home-court advantage. The Cavaliers were still on a high from their playoff showing of 2006. Simply making the playoffs and winning one series was not good enough in the players' minds this time. They wanted more. They wanted a bigger reward. Few experts expected it, but the Cavaliers believed in themselves and felt they could make a run at not only the Eastern Conference title, but the NBA title.

NOTES

1. Tom Withers, Associated Press, November 12, 2006.
2. Branson Wright, *Cleveland Plain Dealer*, December 10, 2006.
3. Channel 3000.com Sports Network, December 9, 2006.
4. K.C. Johnson, *Chicago Tribune*, December 12, 2006.
5. K.C. Johnson, *Chicago Tribune*, December 31, 2006.
6. LeBron James, press conference, Quicken Loans Arena, November 9, 2006.
7. LeBron James, press conference, United Center, December 30, 2006.
8. Kirk Hinrich, press conference, United Center, December 30, 2006.
9. James, press conference, December 30, 2006.
10. Mike Brown, press conference, December 30, 2006.
11. James, press conference, December 30, 2006.
12. James, press conference, December 30, 2006.
13. James, press conference, December 30, 2006.
14. Michael O'Shea, *Parade Magazine*, "The Easiest Way to Shape Up For Life," January 7, 2007.
15. Frank Dell'Appa, *Boston Globe*, January 4, 2007.
16. Dell'Appa, January 4, 2007.
17. Dell'Appa, January 4, 2007.
18. Dell'Appa, January 4, 2007.
19. NBA.com, January 5, 2007.
20. Associated Press, January 6, 2007.
21. Mary Schmitt Boyer, *Cleveland Plain Dealer*, January 25, 2007.
22. Associated Press, January 26, 2007.
23. Branson Wright, *Cleveland Plain Dealer*, January 29, 2007.
24. Bill Livingston, *Cleveland Plain Dealer*, February 18, 2007.
25. Schmitt Boyer, January 25, 2007.

Chapter 11

STEPPING UP TIME

Sometimes a 48-minute NBA game can seem like a lifetime. When the lead see-saws and the score remains close, a few seconds of playing time can be magnified and provide the illusion of lasting minutes. One team can appear to dominate, but a few shot misses, a few bad bounces, and what seems to be a decided game remains tight entering the last stretch.

Not long after the All-Star game, LeBron James and the Cavaliers played one of those games against the New Orleans Hornets. The Cavs held a 12-point lead and were comfortable with the margin. But then things went sour offensively and the Hornets crept back into contention. It remained for James, who was putting in his sixth straight tremendous performance following the All-Star break, to take back the game. James scored 35 points and Cleveland prevailed, 97–89. James, who usually tries to slash to the hoop late in games for lay-ups, seeking to get fouled, instead fooled the Hornets' defense by throwing up long-range, three-point attempts. He sank two of them in the game's last 49 seconds and Coach Mike Brown likened the finish to a baseball player taking a big swing and hitting a home run.

The result and the way the game unfolded were other reminders that not all regular-season games are created equally. They may count the same in the standings, but either because of opponent, timing, conference rivalry, or simply because of how a game is played, some seem to be worth more mentally. The victory over the Hornets fit that bill. Losing after being ahead by 12 points would have been unacceptable and the win moved Cleveland to a record of 33–24, nine games over the .500 mark. Not too many years before the only way the Cavs would see .500

was through a telescope as if it were a mystery planet in a distant solar system. James, who had been scoring less than the season before, posted a 30.5 points average in the six games immediately after the Vegas break. "I've been playing great basketball since the All-Star break individually," he said. "I feel the best I've felt all year. I'm going to try to lead this team the right way."[1]

James's inspired play came at the right time. Mid-season evaluations from some reporters questioned whether he had improved as a player and raised the question of whether he might have hit a wall. The more astute players around the league did not jump to those conclusions. They looked closely at who was playing with James and realized the supporting cast was stronger. That meant James did not have to score as many points every night. "What I see him doing is just taking that next step as a leader for his team," said Dallas Mavericks guard Jason Terry before the clubs met. "He's trying to get all those guys involved and he's not trying to dominate the ball as much as he has in past years."[2]

Dallas was the hottest regular-season team in the NBA during the 2006–07 season, overwhelming many clubs with its balanced offense, its potent scoring ability, and the high-caliber play of star forward Dirk Nowitzki. Dallas brought a 13-game winning streak into its March 1 game against Cleveland, and had gone 48–5 after a surprising 0–4 start. The Mavericks were the talk of the league, putting on a team performance that was the envy of all others. "They're definitely playing out of this world," James said. "They've won 20 straight games at home, and they're like 45–4 or some crazy number since the start." James said the way things were going Nowitzki should be the league's MVP.[3]

It was a measuring stick game. If the Cavaliers could beat Dallas when Dallas was the hottest team around, it would say something. Cleveland, however, was playing without guard Larry Hughes and forward Damon Jones, who were out with injuries. Playing short-handed was a handicap, but Cleveland was heartened by a 95–92 loss on the Mavs' home court. James was in the mix during the last-minute struggles. The Cavs chased the Mavericks to the finish line. James was knocked to the floor on a foul with 10 seconds left and hurt his back. He missed both free throws and a long-range jumper. It is impossible to be the hero every night. "I tweaked my back a little when I went into the fans," James said. "I wasn't able to get as much lift as I wanted to from the free-throw line. I rushed them."[4]

Neither James nor his teammates seemed distraught about this loss, however. They had gone to the wire against the league's best team with a road court disadvantage and with two of their regular players sidelined. If they could play that well every night against all other opponents they might achieve some heady goals before the end of the season. "The effort was awesome," James said. "This is the type of energy and effort we need from everybody. We were short-handed, but everybody played well and tried to get it done."[5]

LOSE AND LEARN

Young professional sports franchises have to learn how to win under pressure and they must learn how to lose with grace. They must also adapt the lessons of losing to the future as they mature to move up in the standings. The wisdom acquired over a few seasons and sharing time with teammates can pay major dividends if a team is smart and talented enough to adjust and apply the experiences of the tough times. That was one reason why the Dallas defeat was a valuable loss. A few days later the Cavaliers crushed the Toronto Raptors, 120–97, treating the dinosaurs like they were unpolished college players. James scored 36 points, but the statistic that spoke loudly about the Cavaliers was their compilation of 25 assists. That meant ball movement was superior and that players were trying to feed teammates who were open rather than force their own shots.

Late in the game the Cavaliers ripped off a 23–7 run. James capped it with two free throws. The misses in Dallas were fresh on his mind and he hit 15 of his 17 freebies against Toronto. "We wanted to make a stamp of approval that we're playing great basketball—and that's what it's about," James said. "We're going into the playoffs strong and it's starting now."[6]

From his first moment with the Cavaliers, James had exhibited the power of positive of thinking in all of his statements about the team, even before they were warranted. He may not have been a college graduate, but James seemed to be an honors graduate of Norman Vincent Peale's course work. Not everyone who listened to James talk at the beginning of the season about how good the Cavaliers were going went along with the program, however. And not every basketball observer was completely sold on James's brilliance. An anonymous scout was quoted through *Sports Illustrated* at around this point of the season saying, "I can't see it happening for Cleveland. LeBron James can turn it on for a couple of games, but I don't see him carrying that team through series after series." This was the opposite of what James preached daily. He did picture himself carrying the Cavaliers through playoff series after playoff series. He had unwavering belief in his own basketball abilities, and he wanted his less-talented teammates to turn to him when in need. He wanted them to count on him when the game was on the line, and he wanted to prove to everyone that he could lead the Cavaliers to a championship.

In the weeks immediately after the All-Star break, James took his game to a new level. If he had seemed less likely to dominate than he had the year before during the first half of the season, those days were gone. He was scoring 30 points almost every night. He was making the big plays on the court every day. One basketball writer summed up James's flourishing game this way: "LeBron James has shifted into a higher gear—warp speed."[7]

James and the Cavaliers had just befuddled Houston and its All-Star center Yao Ming. The best of James was on display in the 91–85 victory when he scored 32 points, with 12 rebounds and 8 assists. And immediately after that, the Cavs bested the Detroit Pistons—in Michigan—101–97 in overtime, with James pumping in 41 points. James said the wins showed that if the Cavs played to their top form they could beat anyone. He might even have been making a believer out of the anonymous scout, who showed no inclination to be outed.

James recognized that he was playing better than he had during the first half of the season and he tried to explain what had changed. "I'm just mentally trying to prepare myself and my team for the playoffs," James said. "I'm trying to execute and find creases and cracks in the defense and trying to read them. Everything has been falling for me, my threes, my mid-range jump shot, my drives, and my teammates are putting me in a comfort level to help me succeed. I've been able to go out there and do some things that I couldn't do early on."[8] Superman was fallible, but it was apparently a temporary condition.

Close games, blowouts, the Cavaliers were winning all types of games, building a solid regular-season record that stood 13 games over .500 at 38–25 in mid-March, second only to Detroit in the 15-team Eastern Conference. Talk was no longer about trying to secure a playoff spot, but trying to secure home-court advantage in the playoffs. The Cavaliers put together an eight-game winning streak in March. But if the Cavaliers were the hottest team, James was not the hottest player in the league. Dazzling Kobe Bryant went on a tear, becoming the second player in league history after Wilt Chamberlain to score 50 or more points in four straight games. Bryant's play even boggled James. "I've always said that Kobe Bryant is the best scorer in our game today, and he's definitely proving himself," James said.[9]

THINKING TEAM

James was always a student of sports history (he is a fan of the New York Yankees in baseball) and had watched film of NBA greats who had preceded him, so it was natural that he had an opinion about Bryant's spree. But James followed the rest of the Eastern Conference teams more closely. He became a scoreboard watcher much like the average fan, keeping track of how Detroit and Chicago were playing. He hungrily sought to add a division championship banner to the Quicken Loans Arena's rafters.

Somehow, during the heat of the race, James also managed to keep an eye on his business portfolio. In rapid-fire succession, off-court action swirled around James, even as he attempted to lead the Cavs to that elusive title. Bunched into a few days at the end of March, it was announced that James had bought a minority ownership in Cannondale, a Connecticut-based bicycle manufacturing company, that James would co-host the ESPYS with comedian Jimmy Kimmel over the summer, and that he was building a mansion in Akron. James already had a Cannondale connection, using the company's bicycles in his annual King for Kids Bike-A-Thon charity event.

Only the day before, James had another get-together with billionaire Warren Buffet. Buffett, 76, turned up in Cleveland to watch the Cavaliers and his new friend James play the Denver Nuggets, Buffet's first NBA game in 60 years, when he was a fan of the original Washington Capitols.

Buffett sat in team seats behind the Cavs' bench. When asked what he and James talked about, Buffett joked that James had asked him to provide some basketball advice and he had asked James for some stock tips.

The ESPYS, organized by ESPN, the cable TV network, radio, and sports magazine conglomerate, are the Academy Awards of sports. James previously won ESPYS for his basketball talent, but the step into co-hosting the 15th annual awards in July represented new territory for him. James had once shunned too much television attention but was easing into becoming a more public figure with his Jon Stewart and David Letterman schmoozing. The ESPYS provided a different forum that, predictably, James said would offer a good time. "I'm really looking forward to it," James said. "It's going to be a lot of fun and a chance to get out there and crack some jokes along with Jimmy." Kimmel immediately began to ham it up about the twosome's partnership. "He's very, very tall," Kimmel said. "I'm not sure everyone knows that about him."[10]

What really got fans talking, though, was the news that James was building a new house in Bath Township, Ohio, about 20 miles south of Cleveland that would make the Quicken Loans Arena look like a pup tent. Set on 5.6 acres of land, the James "crib" as it jokingly was referred to, is 35,440 square feet. Plans indicated it would contain a theater, a bowling alley, casino, barbershop, sports bar, and an aquarium, providing a wide variety of recreational opportunities to chill out. King James was constructing his palace, a castle definitely fit for a king.

For all of the extracurricular goings-on in James's life as the end of the NBA regular-season approached, he did not lose sight of the most important business. When the Cavaliers faced the Indiana Pacers at the start of a five-game road trip, James threw Coach Mike Brown out of the locker room and conducted a players-only meeting. The Cavs disposed of Indiana, 105–94, and clinched a playoff berth. That is what team leaders do—lead on and off the court. "This is my team," James said. "That's my responsibility to make sure everyone's on course."[11]

The Cavs were on the right course from game's start and so was James, who scored 26 points, grabbed 7 rebounds, and passed off for 6 assists. Little life developments like hosting the ESPYS and poring over construction plans for a 35,000-foot-plus mansion were not permitted to be distractions.

STRETCH RUN AND PLAYOFF FUN

LeBron James loomed large on the cover of the April 2007 issue of *SLAM*, the basketball magazine, taking a crossover step, dribbling the ball high behind his shoulder with a fierce look on his face. The cover teaser read, "Bron is the One." The theme of the story was that the Cleveland Cavaliers and the NBA were counting on 22-year-old LeBron James to be all grown up—and he was showing that he had indeed grown up since first being noticed as a 14-year-old. The point was that James was now a man, not an on-a-learning curve teenager. "Lucky for Cleveland—and the League, Bron is up to the Challenge" was the headline. The introduction to the story was also illustrated by a photograph of James from behind, naked from the waist up, with the tattoo "Chosen 1" stretching from shoulder to shoulder.[12]

The article was aptly timed. James was leading the Cavaliers back to the playoffs and the team was determined to make more explosive noise than it had the year before. As long as Cleveland kept playing, James's face was going to be all over national television for the next month or two. Nike, James's main sponsor, had erected a large billboard in downtown Cleveland, an inescapable, monstrous, building-tall message board for James reading "We Are All Witnesses." The idea had caught on that sports fans were witnessing something special. When Warren Buffett attended a Cavs game to watch James play, even he wore a "Witness" T-shirt.

"One of the secrets of the NBA is that for a team to be successful— more specifically, for the supporting players on a team to be successful," the *SLAM* story said, "one of the members of the team has to be willing to sit back and take the attention." In his fourth season in the league, James understood the concept and put himself out front to take the heat and absorb the pressure. "Look, I'm the leader of the team," James said. "When you want to become a real leader, you can't just lead by example. You have to be able to voice your opinion, you have to be able to say things to your teammates and they have to be able to say things back to you. So I can't be quiet. My rookie year I wasn't the leader of the team. My second year I was still trying to learn, and toward the end of last season I started to become more of a leader."[13]

LEADER OF CAVALIER NATION

All of this discussion about James being a leader was shoved to the fore-front of press conferences and interviews because the NBA's second season was about to start. The 82-game regular-season sorts out the pretenders and the contenders, leaving challengers and champions when playoffs begin at the end of each April. One at a time, teams that achieved some measure of satisfaction by reaching the playoffs are eliminated. The last two teams standing, the survivors, one from the East and one from the West, play deep into June while the rest of their friends and competitors sit home watching on TV.

James admitted that if the Cavaliers did not make the playoffs (not something to be feared late in the year), the season would be a disaster. But while basketball writers and fans dismissed Cleveland's chance to go all the way, that's not how James felt. "If I don't believe we can win the title, then it's time for me to get out of this game," he said.[14]

The biggest worry for James and the Cavs was keeping the star healthy. At the very beginning of April, with about three weeks left in the regular season, James battled a tendonitis-plagued knee and missed a game. But after two more days of rest, James played and destroyed Minnesota with 31 points, 12 rebounds, and 6 assists in a 101–88 Cavs win. James said he was only at about 80 percent of full efficiency. James said rehab work, rest, and staying away from contact had paid off.

In a reminder game, the Cavaliers swept through Chicago and defeated the Bulls once more, 112–108 in overtime. The focus continued on keeping divisional opponents at bay. Neither team was going to catch the De-troit Pistons, but either Cleveland or Chicago would end up with the second seed in the East. The Bulls had a four-point lead in the last minute of regulation time and couldn't hold it. James made a three-point play on a drive, a free throw with 42 seconds left, and he leaned in for a 9-foot jumper with 20.7 seconds left. James finished with 39 points. "We showed our mental toughness and got the job done," James said.[15]

When James broke in with the Cavs, then-Coach Paul Silas was impressed enough with his ball handling to try the player out at point guard. In a game against the New Jersey Nets in mid-April, James tried something else fresh. Playing more like a center than a guard or forward, James repeatedly showed off unstoppable post-up moves. James focused on dribbling into the low post then turning and firing. The strategy worked in a 94–76 triumph and James scored 35 points. Although the approach was something new for James, it just added to the aura that he can do anything well on the basketball court. Cavaliers coach Mike Brown enjoyed watching James's change-of-pace moves and said it was a tremendous benefit to the team. It made him wonder if James could make those moves every game.

Normally, James enjoys driving to the basket for dunks and lay-ups, or taking jump shots, but using post-up moves emphasized his physical strength and inside quickness, another skill set. James said he went after so many post-up situations because that's what the defense allowed him. "I took advantage of that," he said. "I'm very comfortable in the post."[16] No one was going to challenge that assertion.

It took until the final day of the regular-season to sort out the Eastern Conference playoff picture. The Cavaliers finished 50–32, the same record as they posted the year before, and claimed the second seed in the conference behind Detroit when the Bulls lost their final game. The Cavs earned the No. 2 seed in the 15-team East and a first-round match-up with the Washington Wizards, the No. 7 seed, in a best-of-seven playoff series.

The Cavaliers spent six months reaching this point. In James's fourth season, the playoffs would decide how far the team had progressed.

PLAYOFF TIME

The Bulls' defeat was handy for Cleveland. Finishing No. 2 positioned the Cavs well. Not only were the Bulls stuck with facing the Miami Heat, the defending NBA champions, they were catching the Heat when previously injured players were on the mend. Cleveland, meanwhile, caught Washington at a time when the Wizards' star guard Gilbert Arenas was sidelined with a knee injury. Caron Butler, another starter, was coping with a broken hand. The breaks of the game all favored Cleveland.

Until the opening game. James took a tumble while driving to the hoop when he stepped on a defender's foot and sprained his left ankle with about eight minutes remaining in the third quarter. Cleveland fans feared that the entire season, so filled with hope, would be ruined. Mike Brown was alarmed. "That made everybody's heart jump a little bit," the coach said. James was in pain, but refused to sit out. Instead, with only four minutes rest, he scored 23 points and collected 9 rebounds and 7 assists. Cleveland won, 97–82. "I had no intention of not coming back," James said. "First game of the playoffs, we've got to set a tone. If I was able to limp on it, I was going to be in there."[17]

When the buzzer sounded, Cleveland led the series, 1–0. The Cavs captured the second game at home, too, and then the playoff moved to D.C. Trying to rev up the home crowd, Arenas and Butler, the injured players, were introduced to the loud fans. But their presence on the bench did not account for nearly what it might have meant if they had been in the lineup. Through the miracles of adhesive tape, ice, and other fundamental care, James bounced back as thoroughly as possible from his sprained ankle. James did give the home fans at Quicken Loans Arena another fright when he did not appear on the court for warm-ups with his teammates. James was undergoing ankle care as long as was practical before he stepped out on the floor with about 13 minutes to game time. If James was at less than full strength, it was not readily apparent. As Cleveland triumphed, 109–102, James scored 27 points and threw in his usual complement of 8 rebounds and 7 assists. The 2–0 lead put the Cavs in control of the series. "Once my ankle warms up, it feels pretty good," James said. "At half-time I'll keep a heat pack on it and use my (rubber) band to keep my ankle flexible."[18] Still, James went through his customary routine for the fans, rubbing white powder on his hands, clapping them together, and sending the particles skyward—Poof!—acting the magician.

The Cavs were determined not to permit the Wizards to steal a game and notch a momentum-changer. James was his usual potent self on the court, netting 30 points and adding 9 assists and 6 rebounds in a 98–92 victory. The Wizards were all but dead.

A few days later, that status report was confirmed. Lacking a pulse or any other sign of life, the Wizards folded their tents for the season as the Cavaliers concluded the series business with a 97–90 victory in Washington. It was the first 4–0 playoff sweep in Cavaliers history and James was the catalyst. In the finale, he scored 31 points and notched 11 rebounds and 7 assists. The Cavaliers showed they were better than they were a year earlier. No one was happier than James and he kept up his one-note campaign speech—that Cleveland was in the hunt to win it all. "Last year," James said, "going into the playoffs, it was all about making the playoffs. We've got bigger and better things now. It's about winning the championship and we're one step closer."[19]

The Cavaliers had adopted a playoff motto—"Rise Up." The theme was flashed on the Quicken Loans Arena message boards repeatedly (although it was never as important or applicable as when James hit the floor with his injury). But that was exactly what the Cavaliers had done in the first round. Cleveland advanced to exactly the same point in James's third season, although with a greater struggle. Yet this victory, the sweep, was more energizing, more impressive. The Cavaliers seemed poised to do more, not merely be stuck on talking about doing more. "The excitement is different this time," Cavs forward Drew Gooden said. "To win in four games and be able to rest and wait for our next opponent, I'll take this any time."[20]

NOTES

1. Brian Windhorst, *Akron Beacon-Journal*, February 28, 2007.
2. Dwain Price, *Fort Worth Star-Telegram*, March 1, 2007.
3. Brian Windhorst, *Akron Beacon-Journal*, March 1, 2007.
4. Branson Wright, *Cleveland Plain Dealer*, March 2, 2007.
5. Wright, March 2, 2007.
6. Branson Wright, *Cleveland Plain Dealer*, March 4, 2007.
7. Tom Withers, Associated Press, March 12, 2007.
8. Withers, Associated Press, March 12, 2007.
9. Branson Wright, *Cleveland Plain Dealer*, March 28, 2007.
10. ABC11TV.com, March 29, 2007.
11. Cliff Brunt, Associated Press, March 27, 2007.
12. Lang Whitaker, *Slam magazine*, "Grown-Ass Man," April 2007.
13. Whitaker, April 2007.
14. Whitaker, April 2007.
15. K.C. Johnson, *Chicago Tribune*, April 1, 2007.
16. Wright, April 13, 2007.
17. Associated Press, April 23, 2007.
18. Branson Wright, *Cleveland Plain Dealer*, April 25, 2007.
19. Associated Press, May 1, 2007.
20. Branson Wright, *Cleveland Plain Dealer*, May 1, 2007.

Chapter 12

CREATING BELIEVERS

Sweeping Washington lifted the Cavaliers' profile around the NBA. The next opponent, New Jersey, loomed as more formidable, but still did not seem particularly intimidating. The way Cleveland—and James—played, most observers considered the Cavs favorites, even if their history did not trend that way. It didn't hurt any that Cleveland had five days of rest before the 2007 Eastern Conference second-round playoff series began and the Nets had 36 hours of recovery time.

The opener was low scoring and not aesthetically pleasing, but the Cavs prevailed, 81–77, despite LeBron James's head cold. The illness played better defense on James than the Nets—limiting him to 21 points and 11 rebounds. But no style points are awarded in the playoffs, only the wins and losses that add up to determining a champion. Cleveland held New Jersey to 37 percent shooting and it was not true that Coach Mike Brown relied most heavily on James breathing infectious air onto the Nets' best players to stop them. Whenever James talked, he sniffled and cleared his throat, but he informed the media that there was never a doubt that he would stay home in bed sipping chicken soup rather than competing in the first game. "It's the playoffs," he said. "You have to battle through it. No matter what it took I was going to be out there."[1]

The heavily sponsored James should have put his agents on the trail of a new endorsement contract for decongestants after he bounced back in the second game of the series with a very healthy looking 36-point, 12-assist effort. James looked cured from his cold as Cleveland toppled New Jersey, 102–92, and with a 2–0 lead inched closer to capturing a second playoff series in a season for the first time in team annals. The Nets executed their offense much more efficiently and forced the Cavaliers into a more up-tempo game while shooting a much better percentage. But it didn't matter. Whenever the Cavs needed a big play, James shook off defenders and made it. "No matter what type of game it's going to be, we believe we can win," James said. "There was a point and time when I was here, if it was a close game in the fourth quarter we would lose, and I learned from that as an individual."[2]

That was a turning point for James as a team leader and for the Cavaliers as a team. They had matured from a team that always lost the close ones into a team that always believed it could find a way to win. After six straight playoff victories, they were proving it to the world, too. Still, no one expected the Cavaliers to sweep every game in this series or to go undefeated in the playoffs. With players like Vince Carter and Jason Kidd, the Nets had too many weapons to go peacefully into the off-season. New Jersey picked off the next game, setting up a crucial fourth game. If the Nets could tie the series anything might happen. If the Cavaliers won, their 3–1 lead would be virtually insurmountable.

Game four was rough. At one point, Cavalier forward Sasha Pavlovic was the recipient of a New Jersey flagrant foul. Even as the referees made the automatic technical foul call to give Pavlovic the two free shots, the situation nearly degenerated into a brawl—with LeBron James, acting the role of protector, in the middle of the fracas. James ended up shouting in New Jersey player Mikki Moore's face up close and personal. If both had been ejected for fighting that would have been a worthwhile trade for the Nets. The Cavs pulled out the close game, 87–85, but James seethed afterwards, denouncing the Nets for picking on Pavlovic for no apparent reason. "It really ticked me off," James said. "They tried to hurt him. And me as the leader, I had to stick up for my teammate. I didn't like it—at all."[3]

If James thought New Jersey would go meekly after falling behind 3–1, however, he was surprised by the way the Nets retaliated in the fifth game in Cleveland. New Jersey was sharper and the Cavaliers reverted to a sluggish form of play that mirrored their undoing in some early-season defeats. During Cleveland's futile chase of the Nets in the 83–72 loss, James battered his right knee as he hurtled into the New Jersey bench, falling over Jason Kidd, and cracking into a chair. James left the game, and the floor, with just under a minute remaining and blood running down his leg.

They might have lost a bit of their swagger, but the Cavaliers still led the series 3–2, a commanding position. They had two chances to end it and advance to the Eastern Conference finals and they hungered to wrap things up in one game. If New Jersey received an infusion of confidence from winning two of the last three games, Cleveland dismissed any suggestion it had any major flaws. Only when the sixth game unfolded in a most aggravating way, with James forced to the bench for long stretches because of foul trouble, did the Cavs worry. Yet the less heralded Cavs, including rookie Daniel Gibson and forward Donyell Marshall, the off-season pickup, helped Cleveland build a 22-point lead. A shockingly troublesome third quarter, with James benched so he wouldn't foul out before the final minutes, left the Nets only one point behind.

James was as distraught as any true blue Cavaliers fan, twitching with anticipation as he sat for long minutes. He couldn't believe it when the Nets ate up almost the whole lead and later said his mind was racing: "Would the third quarter please end so I could get back in the game?"[4]

With James back in the game, New Jersey never gained the lead. James scored 23 points, with 8 rebounds and 8 assists, to move the Cavaliers its deepest into the playoffs since 1992. When the Cavaliers began the next series against favored, top-seeded Detroit, they would be one of only four NBA teams left with a chance to win the 2007 crown. In the preseason, James said he wanted to win a title, but above all he wanted the Cavaliers to advance further in the playoffs than they had since his arrival. That goal was met. "It's a great feeling," James said. "This is one of the best feelings I've ever had as a basketball player."[5]

BRING ON DETROIT

Cleveland made waves in the basketball world by winning two straight playoff series. But the so-called smart money experts did not see the Cavaliers winning another. The Pistons were thought to be too talented, with too much experience and motivation to be conquered by what many still considered to be a one-man LeBron James team. Even James's teammates still acknowledged that perception and recognized that if it turned out to be reality they could not run with Detroit. "We understand that one guy is not going to beat a team of five," Cleveland forward Damon Jones said.[6]

Detroit compiled the best regular-season record in the East. Detroit had the deepest bench and the best one-through-five talent in the East. The Pistons won the league title in 2005. But the Cavaliers were neither scared of Detroit's resume nor intimidated by the personnel. Basketball watchers conceded James more props all of the time, crediting him with lifting the Cavaliers and no longer capping just how far he could carry them.

"LeBron James, he's the face of the NBA," one ESPN announcer said as the Detroit series warmed up.[7]

"It's not often a pro athlete needs to be more selfish, to ignore his teammates and grab some glory for himself," an Associated Press writer proclaimed. "It's even rarer when that athlete is a superstar, for whom entitlement is pretty much a birthright. LeBron James, though, isn't your average superstar. He's polite. He's humble. He plays well with others. Admirable qualities, to be sure—but not at this time of year."[8] The message was clear—Go get 'em, LeBron.

The Pistons had seen it all, however, and their roof wasn't going to fall in merely because of the windy LeBron hype. Detroit, with home-court advantage in the seven-game series, stifled the Cavaliers in the opener, 79–76. Neither James, who scored just 10 points, nor his teammates, looked like contenders. James's actions in the closing seconds of the game supported the AP writer's opinion. Instead of taking the last shot, he passed to Donyell Marshall, who missed a three-pointer. Hence, the thought that maybe James had to be more selfish, had to keep the ball in his own hands in those circumstances, despite the two defenders converging on him. Marshall was wide open. He just missed the shot. James said he made the right choice. "I go for the winning play," he said.[9]

Winning plays were in short supply for Cleveland. Game two shaped up similarly. The Pistons won by the same margin, 79–76, once again containing Cleveland's offense and limiting James to 19 points. Quickly, the Cavs were behind 2–0 and needed to win four of the next six games. Maybe this was the ceiling for this Cleveland team. Maybe this was as far as James could take these Cavs.

The series moved to Cleveland for the pivotal third game. This time the 20,562 fans in Quicken Loans Arena got what they came for. James was James at his best, scoring 32 points and he was the pivotal guy in an 88–82 victory. There was no panic in Detroit, but there was relief in Cleveland.

Detroit's alarm bells started sounding with the insistence of a tornado warning system when the Cavs held off the Pistons to capture the fourth game, 91–87. What had seemed likely to be a walkover, was suddenly an even series. Demonstrative Detroit forward Rasheed Wallace ripped his game jersey off and slammed a wall with his hand when the result was in. Guard Chauncey Billups insisted that the Pistons' confidence wasn't shaken. But the James Gang had done it again and instead of looking at 3–1 with the series almost in the bag, Detroit was looking at 2–2 and wondering what was going on. James posted his routinely brilliant statistical line—25 points, 11 assists, 7 rebounds. In cold, hard numbers, the series was knotted. But in emotion and momentum, the series had tilted to the Cavaliers. "I'm more focused than I've ever been in my life," James said.[10]

All season it had been accepted with little debate that the best teams in the NBA—the Dallas Mavericks, the San Antonio Spurs, and the Phoenix Suns—were playing in the Western Conference. Yet postseason excitement was brewing in the East. Even players on teams already eliminated for the season appreciated James's singular ability to turn his team into something special in just four seasons. "He believes in his teammates when they don't even believe in themselves," said long-time pro Jalen Rose. "And the athleticism! He's only 22 years old. LeBron James is doing it from the ground up."[11]

James showed up at The Q, his home arena, three hours before the fourth game to work out. He shot extra shots and ran himself into a sweat. During the game he drove the crowd into a swooning, applauding, hoarse frenzy, feeding reborn rookie Daniel Gibson for big jumpers and driving past double-teaming defenders while shifting the ball in his hands as a prelude to a tomahawk jam. James moved at an otherworldly pace, making such quick moves to the hoop that some Detroit defenders were left flat-footed, unable to challenge his spins. After Gibson fed James for a high flying, alley-oop dunk, James landed with his knees bent, hands at his sides, and howled from a crouch. Then he pointed to Gibson, an acknowledgment for the sweet pass.

THE NEW NATIONAL HOOPS DARLING

The world of basketball changed in the next game. For years, James had been nicknamed King James. For years, the hardest-to-please critics admitted that he was a good basketball player morphing into great. It was too early, they protested, to advance James into true superstardom until he either led his team to an NBA title or otherwise distinguished himself in a high-stakes game.

Game five of the Detroit series was the moment. Playing as fiercely as they could, the Pistons and Cavaliers arm-wrestled for 3–2 supremacy throughout 58 sublime minutes of basketball before Cleveland triumphed, 109–107 in double overtime. It was James who broke the Pistons' will by transcending earth-bound players and solo accomplishment. James scored 48 points, including his team's last 25 in a row and 29 out of the Cavaliers' last 30 points, along with his 9 rebounds and 7 assists. Never again would it be suggested that James passed off at the wrong time, that he was too unselfish. He took the burden on his shoulders when necessary. His showing left the most seasoned NBA watchers groping for compliments.

"That was a phenomenal performance," Cavs Coach Mike Brown said. "He did it all. This is the single best game I've ever seen at this level, hands down."[12]

It seemed that every bit of LeBron James's celebrity, from the moment he was discovered in summer AAU ball and playing for St. Vincent-St. Mary, led to this virtuoso performance.

"It was amazing," said former NBA star and coach Doug Collins, a TV commentator.[13]

"Some of the things he does are like in a video game," teammate Scott Pollard said. "You think, 'You can't do that in real life.'"[14]

But James could. That night and the next day, James was the talk of radio and television sports shows. He heard more praise than a bride on her wedding day. All day fans ran around saying, "Did you see it?" See it? There was no way to avoid highlights and descriptions of James's magnificence.

The win gave the Cavaliers a third straight playoff victory over Detroit. It was noted that there was one game to go, but few doubted now that the Pistons were going to be dead on arrival for game six in Cleveland. They were. The Cavaliers won, 98–82, to earn their first trip to the NBA Finals. Quicken Loans Arena was party central, the hub of a city's joy. When the final buzzer sounded, Cavalier players celebrated on the court, pulling on ready-made "Champions" baseball caps and T-shirts. They hugged and fans with long memories recalled that the last time any of their professional teams had won anything it was the Browns in 1964.

James, known to smile for much less reason, had a big grin plastered on his face, but seemed dazed by the "Rise Up" accomplishment. Almost no one predicted the Cavaliers would still be contesting meaningful games in June. "This is like a dream," James said.[15] "If I could put into words what's going on in my head, I'd be here for another three hours," he added. "This is special. This is definitely a big step in Cavaliers' history."[16]

It was almost an unfathomable step. So soon after the rebuilding Cavaliers drafted James they were only one step from the NBA championship. Only a showdown with the San Antonio Spurs stood as a barrier.

SUMMERTIME BLUES AND SUMMERTIME HIGHS

Life was wild and crazy in Cleveland. For the first time in the history of the franchise, the Cavs were on their way to the NBA Finals. No one thought they could do it—except for perhaps LeBron James. No one thought they could tackle San Antonio, either (whether the Cavs had beaten the Spurs that one regular-season time way back in the beginning of the season or not), but for the moment that did not matter.

Life With LeBron—as had been fervently hoped—was way better than Life Before LeBron. Only a few years earlier, the Cavaliers were a league joke. Now they were playing for the right to be crowned the best. Surreal. Unreal.

Few communities were as hungry for a professional championship in any sport as Cleveland. So starved for success and sports respect were the residents that simply reaching the Finals carried as much impact for the city as winning it all might mean for another town. It didn't matter who the Cavaliers faced in the Finals, there was a growing sense the LeBron-led club was a team of destiny. It was acknowledged that the savvy Spurs were more experienced, that the confident Spurs already owned three titles, and that the Spurs possessed their own elite superstar player in Tim Duncan. But the Cavaliers had a player's chance, meaning they were in the game and no other team could say the same. They also had the LeBron James X factor. James was playing just about the best basketball of anyone on the planet. If the Cavaliers had deficiencies compared to the Spurs, maybe James could make up for them.

During the short break between series, Cleveland's optimism was at its peak. Once the games began, however, every indication pointed to San Antonio dominance. San Antonio won the opener, 85–76. Then the Spurs won the second game, 103–92. There it was, just as in the Detroit series—Cleveland trailed 2–0. Tim Duncan, guard Tony Parker, and Manu Ginobili controlled the pace and the offense. The Spurs showed more sophisticated defenses than Detroit, bottled up James, and led at every quarter mark in the first game. San Antonio led by 25 points at halftime in the second game. From the start, the series appeared to be a mismatch, although James still talked a good fight. "We're definitely still confident," he said. "It doesn't matter if you lose by one or 30 with us. We've been down 2–0 before."[17]

CLOSE BUT NO CIGAR

It never got any better in the Finals for the Cavaliers. Delusions of victory were fleeting. The Cavaliers battled in game three, but San Antonio pulled out the win, 75–72, for the 3–0 series lead. No NBA team in history trailing 3–0 in a seven-game series came back to triumph. The close call in Cleveland was a virtual seal-the-deal win for the Spurs.

The Cavaliers sought to ignore the big-picture circumstances and played the fourth game with the liveliness of spirit they showed most of the season and that had rescued them against the Pistons. As outstanding as James was versus Detroit, the Spurs used a shifting, versatile defense to contain him. The Cavaliers couldn't even steal one game. The Spurs were focused on business and posted the sweep with an 83–82 victory.

Spurs players got to hoist the championship trophy in Quicken Loans
Arena. Neither individual games nor the series was close enough for Cavs
players to philosophize about what-ifs. They simply got beat. James was
the spark who gave Cleveland hope, but he either ran out of his magic
dust a week too soon or reached the limits of his and his team's capabilities for the moment.

"They have a dynasty already at work," James said. "They don't have
the greatest athletes in the world, they don't have the greatest shooters in
the world, but they probably have the greatest team in the world."[18]

The comments summarized the words LeBron James, recognized as one
of the top basketball players in the world, still longed most to hear said
about his own Cleveland Cavaliers. He was on his way home for the season in mid-June, but already thinking about how to make the future even
better. "You don't want to make the Finals one year and not get an opportunity to play next year," James said. "If we work to prepare ourselves for
next year, and the years to come, we'll give ourselves an opportunity to be
a part of this again. Every team wants to be a part of this."[19]

When a player runs out of games, there is more time to think, more
time to reflect on what happened and how to prepare for the next season.
James did his best to relax. He had joked that he was going to farm out
two-year-old LeBron James Jr. to grandparents during the playoffs so he
could get some sleep. But the night before the final game James and his
girlfriend Savannah Brinson had a second baby boy, Bryce. James lobbied for naming the lad Maximus, as in the main character of the movie
"Gladiator," but Brinson vetoed it and Maximus became the kid's middle
name. James was a dad twice over.

Despite the defeat, James's trademark smile crept back onto his face.
In early July, the Harris poll announced that James was fifth in popularity among American male sports stars—golfer Tiger Woods was No. 1.
Derek Jeter, the New York Yankee shortstop, was second, giving rise to
the thought that perhaps there was ballot box stuffing going on in the
much larger city. When it came to box office, however, an ESPN magazine
analysis indicated that James represented big-time money in the bank for
the Cavaliers.

The story suggested that James was the Most Valuable Player in the
NBA, not merely because he was a top-of-the-line star. In a sport that is
often called a business, the magazine pulled together some business-like
numbers. Since the arrival of James in Cleveland, the value of the Cavs
franchise had increased from $222 million to $380 million, attendance was
up about 9,000 fans per game, and TV ratings were up 300 percent, it was

reported. The Chosen One indeed. "Thank you, your Royal Highness," the story stated.[20] A few people in the Cavaliers' front office smiled, too.

WAIT TILL NEXT YEAR

James was tired and sore at the end of the season. He made good on his preseason promise to lead the Cavaliers to a better finish than the year before. Within a month after the last ball was dribbled, he was back to being LeBron James, the celebrity, the star, the marketing genius when he hosted the ESPYS with comedian Jimmy Kimmel.

The ESPYS, created by ESPN, serve as the Oscars for sports, utilizing fan votes to select the best player, game, and moment in many sports. But the show is as much TV show as sport, and it was a gamble for the network to place the comparatively big-name, but show-biz-limited, James in a starring role.

On more than one occasion James made fun of himself in skits, including singing and dancing as a James Brown sort-of-look-alike to rewritten rap song words spoofing his life. But the lasting image of James on stage followed his introduction by Kimmel who asked the audience to welcome "Just a regular kid from Akron, Ohio."

The curtain parted and King James appeared, wearing a crown, sitting on a throne, wrapped in royal robes, clutching a scepter, as a team of Roman era-clad retainers carried him into the spotlight. The regular kid from Akron, Ohio had come a long way from his homeless days shuttled between apartments by a frightened young mother. In a handful of years, LeBron James had become the ruler of all he surveyed, and those who applauded him on this night seemed as much subjects as fans.

Kimmel took the gag one step further when James alighted from his throne, bending to one knee and kissing James's right hand. He quipped, "Imagine if you had won one game in the finals."[21]

After four years of incredible acclaim, riches banked beyond imagination, and one sprint to a near-championship, the season just completed was a reminder that LeBron James still had at least one goal unmet. Winning four games in the finals was on his mind.

After resting for a few short weeks, James joined Team USA for its critical FIBA Tournament of the Americas competition in Las Vegas. For the United States to participate in China in 2008, the team had to advance out of this zonal play.

This group of all-stars, featuring James, Kobe Bryant, and Carmelo Anthony, took the assignment seriously and swept to the gold medal, ensuring the U.S. presence in Beijing. Crushing Argentina, 118–81, the Americans played intensely and dominated the event.

James more than earned his gold medal, scoring 31 points in the championship game. Game by game the Americans with the biggest basketball reputations in the country shared the ball, took turns leading the scoring chart, and displayed the type of unselfishness that will be needed for them to overcome challenges in China.

"I learned that players can throw their egos and personal accolades out the window," James said. "We came here for one reason and that was to get the gold medal."[22]

Still, there were several times, such as in the title game itself, when James shined the brightest. "You don't like to single guys out," said Team USA coach Mike Krzyzewski, also the Duke University coach, "but LeBron's performance today was one of the best ones in an international game that a U.S. player has had. He was big-time today."[23]

James was a crowd pleaser on another front before NBA teams adjourned for training camps. He was the guest host for the first show in the new season of "Saturday Night Live," the long-running satirical comedy review.

In one skit, James grabbed a piece of chalk, drew some diagrams, and spoofing presidential candidates, announced, "That's how you fix our health-care system. It's not that hard."

During his opening monologue, James again showed his ability to laugh at himself. He introduced himself to the non-sports-fan members of his audience by mentioning his affiliation with the Cavaliers. For all of you who do not follow basketball, he said with a straight face, Cleveland had swept the San Antonio Spurs. "For those of you who do, be cool and shut up. Don't ruin it for everyone else."[24]

As James began preparations for his fifth NBA season, he could proudly point to achievements on and off the court. He had lived up to the promise shown as a dominating high school basketball player by becoming one of the top scorers in the best basketball league in the world. He had contributed mightily to his country's international basketball success. And he had virtually single handedly revived the moribund Cleveland Cavaliers financially, artistically, and with hard-won results.

Given that James began his NBA career at 18 and played well from the start, he has the chance to compile some of the grandest statistics ever associated with a basketball player if he continues uninterrupted by injury. And given how quickly he improved the fortunes of the Cavaliers, James could well be looking forward to a career highlighted by several championships. He is on a path that will lead him to being acknowledged as one of the best ever to play the game.

James had also made himself one of the most recognizable sports figures in the nation and through commercials and televised appearances was crossing over into mainstream America as a performer.

In the sense that James had overcome a difficult upbringing and early-life poverty to become a rich, famous athlete admired by many, his is the quintessential American success story.

NOTES

1. Associated Press, May 8, 2007.

2. James Walker, *Columbus Dispatch*, May 9, 2007.

3. Associated Press, May 16, 2007.

4. Brian Mahoney, Associated Press, May 19, 2007.

5. Tom Canavan, Associated Press, May 19, 2007.

6. Canavan, May 19, 2007.

7. Michael Kay, ESPN radio, May 22, 2007.

8. Nancy Armour, Associated Press, May 22, 2007.

9. Larry Lage, Associated Press, May 22, 2007.

10. Brian Windhorst, *Akron Beacon-Journal*, May 30, 2007.

11. Jalen Rose, ESPN radio, May 29, 2007.

12. Mary Schmitt Boyer, *Cleveland Plain Dealer*, June 1, 2007.

13. Schmitt Boyer, June 1, 2007.

14. Schmitt Boyer, June 1, 2007.

15. Tom Withers, Associated Press, June 3, 2007.

16. Branson Wright, *Cleveland Plain Dealer*, June 3, 2007.

17. Sam Smith, *Chicago Tribune*, June 11, 2007.

18. Tom Withers, Associated Press, June 14, 2007.

19. Branson Wright, *Cleveland Plain Dealer*, June 15, 2007.

20. Peter Keating, "LeBron Came Up Short in the Finals, But He's Still Money for the Cavs," *ESPN The Magazine*, July 2, 2007.

21. ESPYs, ESPN cable television, July 15, 2007.

22. ESPN.com, Sept. 2, 2007.

23. ESPN.com.

24. "Saturday Night Live," TV show, Sept. 29, 2007.

Appendix

CAREER RECORDS

LeBron James's Professional Statistics with Cleveland Cavaliers

Year	Games	Minutes	FGA	FGM	PCT.	FTA	FTM	PCT.	REBS	AVG.	ASST	BLKS	PTS	AVG.
03–04	79	3122	1492	622	.417	460	347	.754	432	5.5	465	58	1654	20.9
04–05	80	3388	1684	795	.472	636	477	.750	588	7.4	577	52	2175	27.2
05–06	79	3361	1823	875	.480	814	601	.738	556	7.0	521	66	2478	31.4
06–07	78	3190	1621	772	.476	701	489	.698	526	6.7	470	55	2132	27.3

Definitions of headings, left to right: year played, games, minutes, field goals attempted, field goals made, shooting percentage, free throws made, free throws attempted, free throw percentage, rebounds, rebound average, assists, blocked shots, points scored, average points per game.

BIBLIOGRAPHY

BOOKS

Cleveland Cavaliers 2006–07 Team Media Guide. (Cavaliers public relations staff).

Gordon, Roger. *Tales from the Cleveland Cavaliers, The Rookie Season of LeBron James.* Champaign, Ill.: Sports Publishing, 2004.

Jones, Ryan. *Believe the Hype—The LeBron James Story.* New York: St. Martin's Press, 2003.

Morgan Jr., David Lee. *The Rise of A Star—LeBron James.* Cleveland: Gray & Company Publishers, 2003.

Robinson, B.J. *LeBron James—King of the Court.* East Cleveland: Forest Hill Publishing, 2005.

Stewart, Mark. *Star Files—LeBron James.* Chicago: Raintree Publishing, 2006.

MAGAZINES

Ballard, Chris, "Now Generation," *Sports Illustrated*, October 23, 2006.

Broussard, Chris, "Don't Let the Smile Fool You," *ESPN The Magazine*, November 6, 2006.

Burns, Marty, "NBA Preview—Cleveland Cavaliers," *Sports Illustrated*, October 23, 2006.

Deveney, Sean, *Sporting News*, December 16, 2004.

Keating, Peter, "LeBron Came Up Short in the Finals, But He's Still Money for the Cavs," *ESPN The Magazine*, July 2, 2007.

O'Shea, Michael, "The Easiest Way to Shape Up For Life," *Parade Magazine*, January 7, 2007.

Platt, Larry, "The Fast Education of LeBron James," GQ, April, 2006.
Time Magazine, "The People Who Shape Our World—The Time 100," April 11, 2005.
Wahl, Grant, "The Chosen One," Sports Illustrated, February 18, 2002.
Whitaker, Lang, "Grown Ass Man," Slam Magazine, April, 2007.

WEB SITES

ABCTV11.com
Canada.com
Channel3000.comSportsNetwork
NBA.com
USABasketball.com

NEWSPAPERS

Armour, Nancy, "LeBron needs to play star card," Mlive.com, May 22, 2007.
Boyer, Mary Schmitt, "Cavaliers Insider," Cleveland Plain Dealer, November 6, 2006.
Boyer, Mary Schmitt, "LeBron Tops All-Star Voting," Cleveland Plain Dealer, January 25, 2007.
Boyer, Mary Schmitt, "All Hail the King's Exploits," Cleveland Plain Dealer, June 1, 2007.
Brunt, Cliff, "Cavs' James Leads With Words, Example," SFGate.com, March 27, 2007.
Canavan, Tom, "Cavaliers 88, Nets 72," San Diego Union-Tribune, May 19, 2007
"Cavaliers Score First Playoff Sweep," Arkansas Democrat-Gazette, May 1, 2007.
"Cavs take Game 1 after holding Nets to 37 percent shooting," ESPN.com, May 9, 2007.
Chicago Tribune Redeye Edition, "James, Jordan Set Record—For Trading Cards," July 26, 2004.
Chicago Tribune, "James Wants Say in Cavs' Free Agent Dealings," June 26, 2005.
Chicago Tribune, "LeBron James Drinking It All In," August 20, 2004.
Chicago Tribune, "James Youngest to 4,000," November 14, 2005.
Chicago Tribune, "Birthday Time for James," December 30, 2005.
Dell'Appa, Frank, "James Times It Right," Boston Globe, January 4, 2007.
Frammolino, Ralph, "Nike Shells Out $90 Million for James," Los Angeles Times, May 23, 2003.
"Home cookin' just fine; James to stay with Cavs," Chicago Tribune, July 9, 2006.
Jackson, John, "Bulls Toss A Clunker," Chicago Sun-Times, November 10, 2007.

"James Scores 35 Points to Lead Cavaliers over Spurs," *Columbus Dispatch*, November 4, 2006.

Johnson, K. C., "James Packing Them in All Over," *Chicago Tribune*, December 27, 2003.

Johnson, K. C., "Don't Give Him His Space," *Chicago Tribune*, November 9, 2006.

Johnson, K. C., "Bawling About Ball Has Impact: NBA Switches Back To Leather," *Chicago Tribune*, December 12, 2006.

Johnson, K. C. "Finishing Off a December to Remember," *Chicago Tribune*, December 31, 2006.

Johnson, K. C. "A Defeat That Can Haunt," *Chicago Tribune*, April 1, 2007.

Krawczynski, Jon, "LeBron James back for Cavaliers," NBA.com, April 3, 2007.

Lage, Larry, "James Takes a Pass on Final Shot, Scores Just 10," *Chicago Tribune*, May 22, 2007.

"LeBron James pours in season high 41 points, Cavs top Pistons 101–97 in OT," Canada.com, March 9, 2007.

"LeBron tweaks ankle, still puts up big numbers in win," ESPN.com, April 23, 2007.

Mahoney, Brian, "James leads Cavs back to East final," globeandmail.com, May 19, 2007.

"Nets push and Cavaliers shove back," USATODAY.com, May 16, 2007.

Price, Dwain, "Cavaliers Young Star Learning To Deal with Great Expectations," *Fort Worth Star-Telegram*, March 1, 2007.

Smith, Sam, "Just Incredible, Michael," *Chicago Tribune*, May 8, 1989.

Smith, Sam, "King James Awaits Reign," *Chicago Tribune*, December 19, 2003.

Smith, Sam, "Athleticism Beyond Belief," *Chicago Tribune*, December 23, 2005.

Smith, Sam, "James Gives Cavs Shot at Bright Future," *Chicago Tribune*, March 1, 2004.

Smith, Sam, "James Comfortable in Spotlight's Glare," *Chicago Tribune*, February 20, 2005.

Smith, Sam, "LJ Better Than MJ? On the Way, At Least," *Chicago Tribune*, May 19, 2006.

Smith, Sam, "Shooting Gallery Is Open," *Chicago Tribune*, June 11, 2007.

Smyth, Julie Carr, "LeBron James Wows Crowd on 'Daily Show,'" cbsnews.com, November 1, 2006.

Temkin, Barry, "Dazzling, Then Writhing," *Chicago Tribune*, June 9, 2002.

Temkin, Barry, "Hyped to the Heights," *Chicago Tribune*, December 6, 2002.

Walker, James, "Cavaliers Can't Close," *Columbus Dispatch*, May 10, 2007.

Windhorst, Brian, "Power Forward, Power Lunch," *Akron Beacon-Journal*, September 21, 2006.

Windhorst, Brian, "LeBron Up to the Task at Crunch Time for Cavs," *Akron Beacon-Journal*, February 28, 2007.

Windhorst, Brian, "Warren Buffett Offers Sage Advice to LeBron James," *Akron Beacon-Journal*, March 26, 2007.

Withers, Tom, "James Rallies Cavs from 19 Points Down," *Columbus Dispatch*, November 12, 2006.

Withers, Tom, "LeBron. James buys stake in cycling company," Newsday.com, March 26, 2007.

Withers, Tom, "James takes Cavs to their first NBA finals," Cleveland.com, June 3, 2007.

Withers, Tom, "San Antonio Downplays Dynasty Talk," *Anchorage Daily News*, June 14, 2007.

Wright, Branson, "What's New? LeBron's Not Having a Ball So Far," *Cleveland Plain Dealer*, November 8, 2006.

Wright, Branson, "Here's One That Didn't Stroll Away," *Cleveland Plain Dealer*, November 10, 2006.

Wright, Branson, "Too Much Pace for Indiana," *Cleveland Plain Dealer*, December 10, 2006.

Wright, Branson, "Hot Foe, Sore Toe, Uh-Oh," *Cleveland Plain Dealer*, January 29, 2007.

Wright, Branson, "No Mercy in Sin City," *Cleveland Plain Dealer*, February 19, 2007.

Wright, Branson, "No Quit, But No Win," *Cleveland Plain Dealer*, March 2, 2007.

Wright, Branson, "James Leads Cavs Romp," *Cleveland Plain Dealer*, March 4, 2007.

Wright, Branson, "LeBron Will Co-Host ESPYs," *Cleveland Plain Dealer*, March 28, 2007.

Wright, Branson, "James Secures Cavs' Win," *Cleveland Plain Dealer*, April 13, 2007.

Wright, Branson, "Cavs 109, Washington 102," *Cleveland Plain Dealer*, April 25, 2007.

Wright, Branson, "Rise Guys," *Cleveland Plain Dealer*, June 3, 2007.

Wright, Branson, "Playoff Rollercoaster Has Matured James," *Cleveland Plain Dealer*, June 15, 2007.

Wright, Branson, "Cavs Enjoy Fantastic Finale," *Cleveland Plain Dealer*, June 19, 2007.

LIVE PRESS CONFERENCES

Mike Brown, Quicken Loans Arena, Cleveland, November 7, 2006.

Mike Brown, United Center, Chicago, December 30, 2006.

P.J. Brown, Quicken Loans Arena, Cleveland, November 9, 2006.

Shannon Brown, Quicken Loans Arena, Cleveland, November 7, 2006.
Kirk Hinrich, United Center, Chicago, December 30, 2006.
LeBron James, Quicken Loans Arena, Cleveland, November 7, 2006,
LeBron James, Quicken Loans Arena, Cleveland, November 9, 2006.
LeBron James, United Center, Chicago, December 30, 2006.
Scott Skiles, Quicken Loans Arena, Cleveland, November 9, 2006.
Eric Snow, Quicken Loans Arena, Cleveland, November 7, 2006.

INDEX